A Portrait of Camphill

A Portrait of

CAMPHILL

From Founding Seed to Worldwide Movement

EDITED BY JAN MARTIN BANG

Floris Books

Some sections of this book were originally published in
Candle on the Hill, published by Floris Books in 1990

This book, first published by Floris Books in 2010, was written
in cooperation with the Karl König Archive, Aberdeen

www.florisbooks.co.uk

British Library CIP Data available

ISBN 978-086315-741-7

Printed in Poland

Contents

Acknowledgments

JAN MARTIN BANG

Like Camphill communities, this book has been created by a cooperative effort carried out by many people on several continents. I would especially like to thank the following: Joan Allen, Francis Aradhya, John Baring, Simon Beckett, Noa Besor, Richard Blake, Friedwart Bock, Hetty v. Brandenburg, Noel Bruder, Tom Burns, Ursula Chowdary, Vashant Deshpande, Wain Farrants, Mischa Fekete, Vivian Griffiths, Colin Haldane, Christof Hanni, Diedra Heitzman, Robin Jackson, Uta Jensen, Ludwig Kraus, Michael Luxford, Neil Maclean, Pete Mernagh, Angelika Monteux, Maria Mountain, Cornelius Pietzner, Andrew Plant, Nick Poole, Russ Pooler, Penny Roberts, Melville Segal, Julian Sleigh, Jonathan Stedall, Richard Steel, Fiona Stuart, Johannes Surkamp and Tho Ha Vinh.

Writing and editing are essentially lonesome occupations, requiring an undisturbed space. I am grateful to my family for supporting me in this, and helping to provide me with the peace and quiet that I needed.

I wish to use this opportunity to thank the wider Camphill world, all those thousands of individuals, members, people in need of help, volunteers and those uncategorized individuals who 'just drop by.' Together you have created something very special in the world, and I hope that this book will in some way record and reflect that contribution. Thank you!

Foreword

CORNELIUS PIETZNER

The world in which Camphill was born is a world that hardly exists today. In 1940, during the ravages of a brutal and devastating war, with the greatest resistance and under the most challenging of life circumstances, Camphill was like a seed implanted in what was a foreign, granite-strewn soil of northern Scotland. Some seventy years later this Camphill seed has taken root, grown, flourished and flowered and propagated into many countries. Perhaps the various elements of early resistance made this seed especially hardy and particularly fertile. This is one important factor in the development of the Camphill 'species.'

Yet, the wider climate conditions for this seed have changed radically in the intervening decades. Indeed, the rate and nature of this change is so fundamental and includes so many different aspects, that completely new conditions may threaten the continuing integrity, at least in its historically recognized form, of this unique impulse.

Clearly, one can take the metaphor only so far. But with legislation, immigration, funding and policy developments, succesion, new education alternatives and changes in social thinking and options, both the external circumstances in which Camphill communities can develop, as well as the more complex and subtle internal, spiritual aspects, will likely encounter significant new challenges in the years to come.

For this reason, too, it is most welcome that Camphill has elected to document its activities and record its remarkable contribution with this new publication.

Dornach, Switzerland, February 2010

Introduction

JAN MARTIN BANG

What is Camphill? Very briefly, it is a worldwide network of communities, inspired by the anthroposophical studies of Rudolph Steiner and his followers such as Karl König, which works with people who need help in their lives. Within Camphill there are two parallel impulses: that of helping others, based upon recognizing that everyone is unique, and has individual physical, psychological and spiritual aspects that make up who they are; and that of creating an alternative society.

In *A Portrait of Camphill* we hope to paint a more vivid picture of Camphill life, to capture the essence of something alive and changing through words and pictures. We describe a good deal of the external aspects of Camphill, but there are also the inner aspects, the soul character, which we attempt to convey.

The Camphill Movement is difficult to define. Camphill is one of the largest and most widely spread community movements in the world. Over the last seventy years, the working of anthroposophy has provided the Camphill Movement with the strength and motivation to spread into over twenty countries. We publish a directory every few years, which includes a list of places and telephone numbers. It is definitive, it has clear boundaries, but the Camphill Movement itself remains fluid: who is in and who is out is not so easy to define (see the introduction to Chapter Five). It's often referred to as an impulse rather than a defined organization.

For those working in Camphill it's important to gain an insight into one's own personal situation. We look into ourselves to try and focus on what motivates us; the events of our daily lives mirror internal events. The Camphill impulse strives to combine esoteric inner work with external social efforts. The spiritual world works through Camphill, encouraging, helping and inspiring us to carry out good works in the world. The founders of the communities met powerful spiritual forces, and focussed strongly on their inner lives. There was always a danger that the outer world would dominate, and that the inner schooling would be overshadowed.

Communities are at heart spiritual creations. They are held together by a web of relationships that spring from the spirit. The material forms — the buildings, the fields, the technology and the economy — are all dependent upon the subtle relationships between the individuals that make up that community. What is the soul component in community? How does it behave? Where did it come from in the first place? We hope to highlight some of these questions in this book.

Intentional community has been a feature of our western civilisation for centuries, as far back as the Essenes in the years before Christ, possibly earlier. Communities seem to have a life of their own, taking ideas and carrying them from generation to generation. Ideas are introduced into the social realm through communities and often live on after communities have disbanded. Some people regard the communal phase as merely the initial period in the life of an idea, which eventually fades away, leaving ideas to establish themselves throughout society. Communal living might be seen as a vehicle rather than a destination.

Many communities are indeed focussed around some higher ideal of improving society or encouraging greater environmental awareness. This may be a collective task in which the individual can, to a certain extent, lose him or herself. These ideals get us up in the morning, and sometimes motivate us to spend all night working together when the need arises.

Do these kinds of ideals have lives of their own, reappearing in different communities as the opportunity presents itself? Are there higher ideals that move from one community to another? If each community has its own spiritual existence, its own group soul, are these related to each other? However far fetched this may seem, it does appear that remarkably similar utopian ideas emerge at regular intervals in different places. These ideals take us out of our own narrow selves, out of our own small village, and connect us to the greater world, to the planet and the cosmos.

Camphill is now celebrating its seventieth anniversary. Is it an older, wiser and more mature movement? Is it capable of further growth and development in a different social context? Will it meet the new challenges presented by today's world?

The book *A Candle on the Hill* was originally published in 1990 to mark the fiftieth anniversary of the founding of the Camphill communities. It became a classic, an advertisement for and explanation of Camphill. Twenty years on, this new, updated version presents the same celebration of Camphill's origins and history; Karl König's life story has not changed, and the excerpts of his writings that end Chapter One are timeless. But in the subsequent chapters we look closely at present perspectives on Camphill and what directions we might find ourselves going in the future.

There is no doubt in my mind that our world faces serious challenges today. Over the past seventy years Camphill has been active in working out solutions to the environmental crisis, to the social and financial crisis, and pioneered new ways of caring for those in need. We live in exciting times. Do the co-workers of Camphill today have the energy to present the world with these solutions? And does the rest of the world have the imagination to recognize these as possible ways forward into the future?

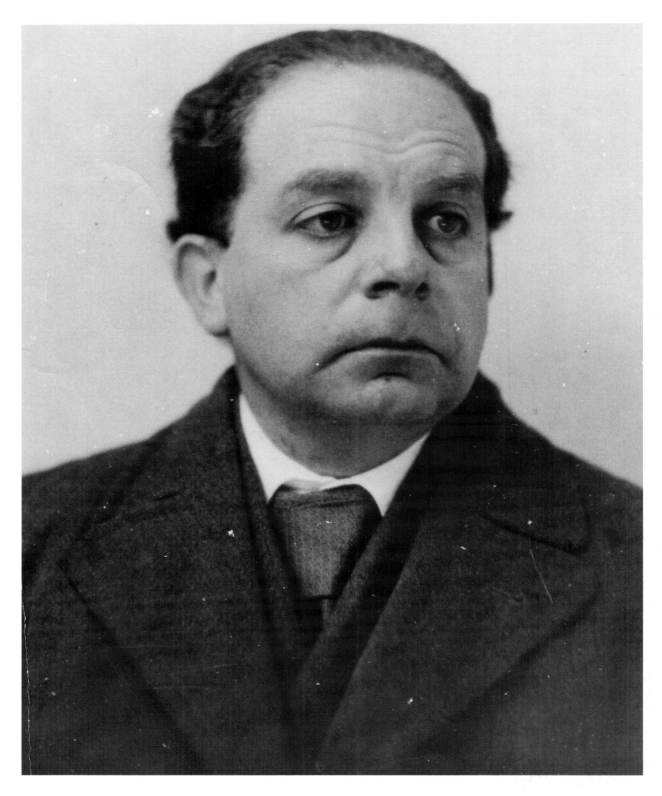

Karl König, founder of the Camphill Movement

1. Karl König

CHRISTOF-ANDREAS LINDENBERG

Karl König's life between 1939 and 1966, and the unfolding and growth of Camphill, is so closely intertwined as to be one story. To relate this part of his biography is also to find the manifestation of an impulse that led to a worldwide movement of homes, schools and villages on four continents. The thought that König was solely responsible for the development of Camphill must be balanced by the very core of the impulse: the idea of community. Thus the story of the founding group of young people who gathered around the Königs in Vienna from 1936 to 1938 is an integral part.

Interrupted in their studies by the annexation of Austria by Nazi Germany, many of the founding group gathered with the Königs in a small manse in North-east Scotland just before the Second World War to work together for an ideal. Then there is the story of those who joined the founding group after the war, and of the many who came to live and work with the growing Camphill Movement as part of their unfolding destinies. Community building is the inherent force in this growth process, which involves many people, not just one man. This introduction gives a picture of one man's unique contribution to Camphill, and its growth in many countries. The development of the Camphill centres is due to all, handicapped or not, who form the living communities. Karl König, however, is rightly referred to as the founder of the Camphill Movement.

Small in stature but great in bearing, Karl König was a controversial figure. What was he like? Many pictures come to mind.

As always for his lectures, the Camphill Hall is filled to capacity. Dr König steps forward, a folder held tightly under his left arm. He walks with customary deliberation to the table. Then he rearranges his space: the glass of water, the flowers, sometimes the position of the table is altered, if only a little, no matter how carefully some of the 'old hands' have prepared everything. Having arranged his books, he clasps his hands behind his back, straightens up as if in a moment of decision, fastens his gaze on a point above the audience, and begins, often in a kind of questioning tone. 'Dear friends, I have the impression that it would be necessary for us to turn to the coming Easter festival ...'

His voice does not dwell on addressing the audience. There is almost no break between 'Dear friends' and what follows, which has the effect of taking the listeners right into the question of the coming seasonal festival. His audience often had the impression that he read these signs from a place behind them, and, as his gaze indicated, a little above their heads.

He shunned figures of speech or intellectual excursions. He was very direct. Often quoting Rudolf Steiner verbatim, he linked these passages with our situation.

Steiner's words became contemporary through König. He demanded our attention and his eyes would flash if somebody interrupted him with a cough, or nodded off to sleep. König was a master at creating imagery that helped us follow his line of thought. He once described the seasons of the year in their outgoing movement from winter to summer, adding the image of arterial blood streaming from the heart to the capillaries. And he compared the descending, centring half of the year toward Christmas to the venous blood returning to the heart. He spoke of the possibility of threshold experiences when going from one half of the year to the other, and the kinds of mental illness which may arise: the schizophrenic tendency in entering the ascending part of the year; the manic-depressive tendency on crossing from the height of summer to the depth of winter. Such images often helped us to deepen our grasp of the concept.

He was also adept at imitating the animals he described, so we had the impression that he actually became the sparrow or squirrel he was talking about. A zoologist at heart, he deemed it a privilege when the opportunity arose to turn to the animal world. He delighted his listeners. Whether in a light or grave mood, most of his talks addressed themselves to our potential to become more awake, useful and essential in our anthroposophical striving. His public talks never failed to inspire moral enthusiasm, often changing people's lives there and then. The person of König and the spoken word were synonymous.

When I think of Karl König the writer, I remember the concentration of his posture, the deliberate way he held his big fountain pen, how his arms bent in an action of utmost intensity. I know that I witnessed a man of will. Through his writing he was in touch with the whole world: he prepared the founding of centres, he startled the experts with his medical papers, he comforted parents and taught out of his knowledge of anthroposophy. One of König's close friends told me how he had managed to get so many people to help with the Camphill Movement: 'He always answered their letter of inquiry quickly.' Indeed, a look at his desk showed that he always seemed to be up to date. To anyone visiting him this was a marvel. To those of us who knew the number of letters and papers he dealt with daily it was beyond comprehension how he accomplished the work.

As early as 1942, when the first Down's syndrome children came to Camphill, König had researched the disease with profound interest. He loved these children and so he pondered the riddle that they pose. Seventeen years later he published the first clinical study to appear in German (Der Mongolismus). Like other pioneers in curative education before him, the enigmas encountered stirred the doctor and humanitarian in him to put questions and investigate ways of helping and healing these children. With new insights, he regularly wrote about children with spasticity, the thalidomide sufferer, and the disturbed conditions he met in the thousands of children that came to him. Apart from itinerant consultations, he had the experience of many children in the community setting of the Camphill schools. By holding conferences with resident or visiting doctors, and working with those who looked after the children, he formulated treatment and educational methods. He fostered meetings where this spirit of inquiry could be shared.

I believe that König wrote all his books in this spirit so they are not his creations alone. This is true not only for the study in child psychology on the order of birth in the family, which was published as *Brothers and Sisters*, when almost every co-worker helped by supplying data, but also for *The Human Soul*, and perhaps his most outstanding book, *The First Three Years of the Child*. His insights were 'ploughed under,' as it were, in seminars, and worked through in a supplementary way by the experiences of others; always linking his creative thought with living reality.

Dr König with a Down's Syndrome child

Karl König documented his wide-ranging interests in hundreds of articles that stretched from his major interest, embryology, to history, human biography and zoology. Many things were written by the medical doctor, by the teacher, and by the research scientist. He also wrote what one could call petitions for the social standing of the handicapped. Other writings were prompted by his ever-growing concern for the suffering of man and the needs of the earth. Attacks on the dignity and integrity of man called him to write and speak. He often wrote long scripts for his lectures, complete with quotations. When giving the same talk in another place, or in a slightly different context, he wrote it out again with a seemingly untiring pen. Here was a man who always managed to link his active thought-life with the will to write.

In contrast stands the artist writer. In quieter moments, or when he was ill, Karl König created poems or lyric stories. Friends put together a volume for his sixtieth birthday which, understandably, leaves out the more personal selection. Among his best works are the festival plays, which still bring the community together in a special way in the season of the year they highlight. König always had a particular cast in mind when writing these dramas, but the plays have been performed successfully by other groups. Some of the plays are more like pageants, involving the whole gathering of people. The most well-known is the St John's play, for midsummer. In it, the players gradually form into a bell, singing, swinging and intertwining; the bell of mankind. The players end in a reconciling circle of oneness. No words can bring close the experience of an unfolding community as do such celebrations enacted in harmony, when the word is lifted to common movement and song.

In September 1952, at his fiftieth birthday celebration in Camphill House, Karl König agreed to play a piano duet with Susi Lissau — a rare pleasure for us. Then he told us that he had never felt that he had aged. As a child and throughout his youth, he always felt himself to be the same unchangeable self. While he assumed this to be a common experience, we realized that it was perhaps more true for him than for others. A photograph from 1927 shows the young man of 25 with the expression of someone in their late forties; deep wrinkles and a moustache complete the impression. Already as a child he had a wise, knowing look in his eye.

Karli, as his Jewish mother called him, was born on Thursday, September 25, 1902, to parents who owned a shoe shop in Vienna. In that year the Swedish educationist Ellen Key proclaimed the twentieth century as the Century of the Child. Well loved and cared for, he nevertheless did not have an easy childhood. Being an only child, born with slightly crippled feet and over-awake in his senses and soul, he looked into the world precociously. There was something special about König as a child. When the two-year-old blond curly-head sat in his pushchair outside the shoe shop, a psychology professor, strolling by, was startled enough to go into the shop and inquire to whom the child belonged. He told the proud mother, 'He will be a very famous man in later life. In my whole career of studying heads I never came across so special a form as this child's head.'

König did not mix much with other children as a growing child, but helped his parents in the shoe shop. Once he said, 'School-time was not altogether smooth-running.' His parents witnessed with concern an all too early independence. They found a picture of Christ in his cupboard when he was eleven years old. Although he celebrated the customary Jewish bar mitzvah at the age of thirteen, he had already begun to find his own way to Christianity.

His social awareness at the beginning of the First World War made him a young St Martin, sharing his cloak with the beggars he saw around him. He refused to eat his mother's home baking when he thought others were starving. He spoke out when he witnessed cruelty to animals, and was arrested by the police for doing so. König described himself as self-willed. He also suffered an increasing number of migraine attacks. As a growing youth, his mother noted, 'There was such sadness in him, as though he had to carry the whole pain of the world alone.' His eyes saw, his ears listened to the dilemma of his time, long before he was a grown man and could do something about it.

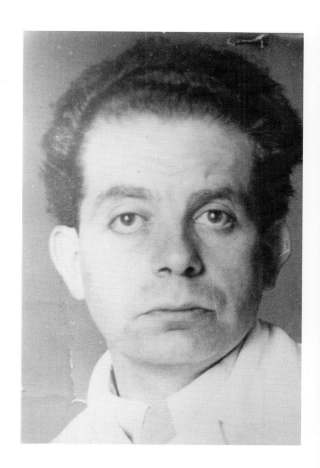

Towards the end of his schooling, Karli was deeply immersed in Haeckel, Freud, Buddha and Lao-tzu, Dumas and Balzac, but especially the New Testament, seeking his way. His library grew when, after a quiet and successful matriculation, the eighteen-year-old studied all the necessary texts for natural scientific research with, he said, 'a primeval force' that came over him. He was then in his pre-medical year. When he was finally led to Goethe's natural scientific writings, he compared his enlightenment with his experience of discovering the New Testament. In 1921 he heard of Rudolf Steiner, and found a group of doctors and students who were discussing Steiner's lectures on the study of man. Then came the important discovery on reading Steiner's *Philosophy of Spiritual Activity*: 'Here is all I myself have noted down on nature's creative force in human thinking.' It was an overwhelming experience. He wanted to meet Steiner, but missed going to his East-west Congress in Vienna in June 1922. He never had another opportunity for the much wished-for encounter.

König the medical student was also a teacher and research worker. For three years he worked at the Embryological Institute of Vienna, and while there, at the age of 23, he published his first research papers. When König graduated in 1927, Alfred Fischel, dean of the university, wished to employ him as an assistant at the Embryological Institute, as long as he would keep anthroposophy to himself, a condition that convinced Dr König to decline the offer. He had become a member of the Anthroposophical Society and would follow a different calling. In the summer of 1927, Dr König gave his first lecture at a public anthroposophical conference. He then worked for some months in a children's hospital, his name rapidly becoming known. And then the call came.

Dr Ita Wegman, leader of the medical section of the Steiner-instituted School of Spiritual Science in Dornach, Switzerland, came to Vienna on a brief visit. Meeting Dr König briefly, she invited him to work at her Clinical Therapeutic Institute in Arlesheim, near Dornach. He accepted at once.

In the weeks that followed, destiny played a significant part. Entering the clinic, he met his future wife, the nurse Tilla Maasberg, who had arrived from Silesia that same November day. Twenty days later, on Advent Sunday, he witnessed the Advent garden and saw severely handicapped children walking with lighted candles in a very special festival. He wrote afterwards, 'In this hour the decision was taken that I would dedicate my life to the care and education of these children. It was a promise I gave to myself: to build a hill upon which a big candle was to burn so that many infirm and handicapped children would be able to find their way to this beacon of hope and to light their own candles so that each single flame would be able to radiate and shine forth.' In the clinic he could deepen the anthroposophical approach to medicine. This work was reflected in a series of articles on embryology, then the foremost subject on his mind. König the writer had emerged.

A little more than four weeks after the Advent experience in the Sonnenhof, König was encouraged by Dr Wegman to hold his first lecture in the makeshift hall of the Goetheanum at Dornach during the Christmas Conference. He spoke on world evolution as reflected in embryological stages of development, based on his recent studies. This successful talk heralded the arrival of König the lecturer and led to a lecture tour to Breslau. This tour was to lead him to the place of his future work. For the next seven years, Karl and Tilla König put all their efforts into the new curative home, Pilgramshain, in Silesia, working with handicapped children. Destiny had spoken, and a life of dedication to the child in need of special care, and to the handicapped person in need of integration, had been born out of those portentous weeks in Switzerland.

Dorothea von Jeetze, who lived for many years in Camphill Copake in America and passed away there in 1993, recalls how Dr König came to Pilgramshain. She tells how he visited a small children's home run by the Maasberg sisters while on his lecture tour. On Ascension day in mid-May, he was seriously asked to work there, but could not imagine practising in such a small place. The same day, Joachim and Dorothea von Jeetze came seeking acceptance of their offer of their nearby mansion house and park at Pilgramshain for the Maasbergs' and A Strohscheins' curative education work. Now König felt doubly attracted, for he was already very connected to Tilla Maasberg and to her Herrenhut (Moravian Brethren) background, and now there was also the offer of a castle and grounds. Great moments call for quick decisions. The curative home in Pilgramshain was started that August, and in September Dr König joined the venture. He married Tilla the following year. As well as acting as doctor for the home, he also built up a medical practice in the area which, in the next seven years, was to draw a large number of patients. The requests for lectures also increased.

Little is written about the years at Pilgramshain, but it is clear that there König developed his medical approach to learning disabilities and organizational insight to residential care. What had to wait for another time was the concept of community, both from a social and spiritual standpoint.

Dr König was 33 when, under political pressure and impelled to search further, he decided to leave Germany. He could not take any money over the border into Austria, and he arrived back in his home town to what appeared to be a new beginning. It turned out to be different. The two year period he spent in Vienna was a time of inner and outer preparation.

The group of young people who gathered around the busy doctor were to become lifelong friends and co-founders, and their enthusiasm was kindled by Dr König's weekly talks and their discussions. Many of them had Jewish backgrounds and they soon felt the pressure of Nazi Germany. On the day of Austria's annexation to Germany, March 11, 1938, they were ready to disperse, but remained bound to each other. That day remains as a kind of eleventh hour for the whole of Europe. The world does not need strategy and outer actions, the future depends on silent deeds performed in mutual recognition, and a minute little band of people left home and country to do that. They were to kindle a community fire which now burns in many countries, and in many hearts.

Dr König could be a difficult person to approach. Yet every time, on entering his room, one was at once reassured by his welcome. He seemed to know you, and in the brief time allotted, mostly half an hour, unspoken doubts were dispelled and superficial analyses of a situation corrected. Meeting him, one felt warmer. This must have been the experience of the many thousands of people who sought his counsel, whether in a personal meeting or by writing to him: the feeling of warmth through being recognized. We often witnessed it when he spoke to children; a bridge of warmth was created in that moment.

Dr König always had a lot of things on his mind. In the course of a day he would meet very many destiny stories, some disturbing matters, be faced with a variety of difficult situations, while having to plan lectures, courses, journeys and confirm the work and direction in the new communities. However, in a private meeting you always met his undivided attention and love. The accompanying challenge to do better was not the main thing you took away, but rather the thought that you had untapped resources for doing infinitely better — an enthusiasm and confidence engendered by the increased flowing warmth. A phenomenon of the Camphill Movement is the uninterrupted growth in the number of people coming to join the work. Dr König had the rare gift of knowing almost all the many co-workers by name. He knew the people who supported the work, the parents, and so very many special children and villagers; and in turn all felt known by this man of the heart. His unbounded human interest penetrated the whole movement. And he always included those who had died.

Near the end of his life, Karl König wrote:

Only the help from man to man — the encounter of Ego with Ego — the becoming aware of the other man's individuality without enquiring into his creed, world conception or political affiliations, but simply the meeting, eye to eye, of two persons, creates that curative education which counters, in a healing way, the threat to our innermost humanity. This, however, can only be effective if with it a fundamental recognition is taken into consideration, a recognition which has to come out of the heart.'
(*Camphill Brief*, Christmas 1965)

It is difficult to imagine the change from Vienna city life to that in a remote granite manse in the north-east of Scotland — out in the windblown countryside, without amenities or electric light. From March 30, 1939, the growing group of Austrian refugees learnt, day by day, to handle broom and hoe and create a home for twelve children in need of special care. Thirteen months later, the men in the group were interned as enemy aliens. During their six-month absence, the women brought about the birth of Camphill. On June 1, 1940, the move into Camphill House and the estate near Aberdeen took place. The way that led from the humblest of beginnings to that spiritually determined beginning is what makes that day a true birthday, and justifies using the name Camphill to cover the whole worldwide movement.

When he was applying for planning permission, Karl König wrote down as the purpose of the intended work: medical, curative-educational and agricultural pursuits. That gave freedom for future development. Long before the Camphill villages came into being, Dr König, Thomas Weihs and others had deepened their knowledge of biodynamic agriculture. König arranged medical conferences for doctors, nurses and therapists, and with the many helping physicians laid a foundation for the gradual development of a science of curative education. This is taught in the International Camphill Seminar held in many countries.

Dr König became ill in 1955. Recovering, he entered the most intense period of involvement in the expanding Camphill Movement. During his last eleven years he was able to help in the threefold ordering of life within the centres, as well as establishing villages and schools in Germany, the United States, Switzerland, Ireland, Holland and Scandinavia. His heart was worldwide, but his focus and will were directed to the immediate surroundings. A fine example of his greatness was his ability to delegate and foster responsibility for the impulse and all realms of work. He gave up his chairmanship of the Camphill Movement, acting as *primus inter pares*. From the beginning, the Camphill work was built, formed and carried by many people. At the end of his life the king in him had fully united with the shepherd. In 1965 he said again that the handicapped children and adults are our true teachers, and that he too was learning daily from living together with them.

I have tried to sketch the man of imaginative thought, the man of determined will, and the man of great heart, to paint a portrait of a unique brother for those in need. Only by surveying the whole development and present position of the Camphill Movement can Karl König's contribution be rightly estimated. Other articles and pictures in this book give a view of the diversity of the work. But it stands out clearly that one man in particular was able to bring down the right thoughts and perform the necessary deeds at the right moment. Thus Karl König, in the years from 1939 until his death on March 27, 1966, was the ongoing founder of the worldwide Camphill Movement indeed.

Camphill essentials

KARL KÖNIG

We men of the present age
Are in need of the right ear
For the Spirit's morning call
St Michael's morning call.
Knowledge of the spiritual world
Will open the portals of the soul
Towards true hearing of this morning call.

Verse by Rudolf Steiner spoken at the beginning of every College meeting.

Dr König repeatedly felt urged to put his experiences into imaginatively formulated thoughts that became spiritual nourishment for others. The following introduction to an essay was written for the Cresset, a Camphill journal, at Christmas 1959. It allows the reader to sense how individual destiny can be woven into the destiny of the community, and from there become part of the tapestry of the destiny of mankind through 'the right ear for the Spirit's morning call.

The Camphill Movement

Christmas 1959 — and it is 21 years ago that I first celebrated this festival here in Britain and not in my own country. I was sitting in a tiny room, in one of the hundreds of back streets of London. Alone, a drop in the vast human sea of a city, a stranger, a foreigner. I knew that with me, tens of thousands of people shared the same fate. Men and women, old and young, children and adults, we were all in the same boat. It was the boat of loneliness; a ship without a destination, a life uprooted from the native soil and barely saved, like a plant which is given a handful of earth in a little pot of clay. How would we survive?

The small candle in front of me lit the few green branches on the mantelpiece and the gas fire hummed a low song. My thoughts went out into the future. Would it be possible to turn this lonely life into order and shape again? Would the fragments of my existence be put together again so that they may build a new frame? I was one of the many who were just too young to be a soldier in the First World War. Then came a time of breathtaking recovery and all seemed to be well when, gradually, a second war appeared on the horizon. And here I was, thrown out of my work and I felt like one who, after a shipwreck, was cast on to a lonely, unknown island.

The flame of the candle jerked and quivered and threw strange shadows on the wall. I had left Europe behind me. Here it was no more the land of Europe; it was a country of the Western World. The language was foreign to me; the people were strangers. Their way of living was not my way and their past was almost unknown to me. I had a different background, different modes of existence, different thoughts. Some of these strangers had turned to me with a friendly gesture. Others, on whom I had previously counted, showed no more interest than just the limits of good behaviour would permit.

I was alone! Would I again have the strength to begin anew? In a few days my wife and children were to arrive and, in several countries on the continent, a number of young friends were waiting to join me. Join me in what? Would I be permitted to work? And if so, what kind of work was I to do? But in Italy and France, in Holland and Switzerland, in Germany and Czechoslovakia, friends were waiting to join me! A house had been found in the north of Scotland where we could start to live together. But what kind of life would we live? It would become only an enclave in this land; we would be strangers in a big community. And what was our task?

The light of the candle now was quiet and bright and my eyes turned to a small book which a kind person had given me as a Christmas present. It was an English Bible; never before had I held one in my hands. I was astonished to realize that the present translation was sponsored by James I, a man and monarch for whom, for many years, I had had the highest esteem. I had learnt to admire this 'greatest fool of Christendom' and I read now the following words in the dedication: '... to go forward with the confidence and resolution of a man maintaining the truth of Christ, and propagating it far and near ...' *Is this not common ground on which I may stand?* I asked myself.

It was common ground. And now I saw and knew some more about the future task which lay before me. I saw Austria overrun and conquered by men who had betrayed the very essence of Europe. They had turned it into a camp of nationalists, searching for might and power. Europe was overcome by their vain glory and was preparing to become a battlefield. Could we not take a morsel of the true European destiny and make it into a seed so that some of its real task might be preserved? A piece of its humanity, of its inner freedom, of its longing for peace, of its dignity?

If this were possible, would it not be worthwhile to live and work again? Let us try to become a morsel of this Europe which, at the moment, had to disappear. But let us not do it in words but in deeds. To serve and not to rule; to help and not to force; to love and not to harm, will be our task. Thus I was thinking.

I understood my thoughts. They had emerged after weeks of trial and need and now stood before me and helped me to clarify my problem of existence. On this Christmas Eve neither Camphill nor the movement existed. The future was shrouded but a will started to find its way.

Threefoldness is the hallmark of every living organism. Throughout the history of Camphill, forces of growth, development and metamorphosis have been experienced that have their foundation in the recognition of a threefold social structure corresponding to man as a being of body, soul and spirit. On the occasion of Camphill's 21st anniversary, Dr König described three great personalities that stood as 'godfathers' to his inspirations: Amos Comenius, Count Zinsendorf, Robert Owen.

The following essay, written in 1965, expresses his fiery convictions drawn from 25 years of community life in the service of those in need of special care; convictions that inspired others.

The three essentials of Camphill

Looking back to the early beginnings 25 years ago, we can observe a slow uphill advance. It is by no means a story of success and splendour. It is a tale of trial and error, of hard labour and of many failures.

25 years is a long time! Much greater things have happened in the course of quarter of a century. But Camphill had to grow against many odds and — to begin with — under rather unfavourable conditions. It has, nevertheless, made its way and will continue to pursue its aims. The goal is still far ahead.

Materially we began with next to nothing. Around us was a foreign country and almost the whole world at war. We — a small band of refugees — were classified as 'enemy aliens' and most of us had to spend many months in an internment camp. After our release the war gathered strength and fury and the country was fully occupied combating a deadly onslaught.

During this turmoil of 'sweat and labour, of blood and human suffering' the seed of Camphill slowly began to sprout. The silent message of the handicapped child reached a number of parents, doctors and teachers. Education authorities heard of our effort and sent some of their charges to Camphill. An increasing number of inquiries reached our office and the available space was soon unable to satisfy the demand.

We, therefore, tried to acquire or rent some neighbouring estates in order to enlarge our work. A few helpers and friends joined the original nucleus of people, but not nearly enough to carry the spreading task satisfactorily. There were far too many children for the handful of co-workers. Only by sheer grace, and the greatest sacrifice on the part of everyone, could this difficult period be surmounted. But gradually relief and help came.

The war changed into peace; frontiers were opened and young people came from the continent to help us. More and more parents, relieved from the heavy burden of the war, supported our efforts, and some influential people gave us advice and counsel. The seed of Camphill had already grown into a small plant. Branches developed and attempted to sprout through their own strength.

And one day, a few buds began to appear on one or other twig of this tiny bush. They unfolded into flowers and radiated their beauty and scent into our hearts. These flowers were the inner victories of our external labour and work: the improvement we observed in some of the children, the peace slowly achieved in daily life, the silent wonder during the services on Sunday

Dr König with Emil Bock (left)

morning, the sudden understanding of the innermost nature of one or another of the children — these were the things that made our work worthwhile.

We gradually became aware of the beauty of these flowers. We began to realize that their radiance gave us strength and perseverance. But there were long stretches of time when the bush of Camphill had no flowers. The leaves of everyday life just continued to grow, but no further fresh buds appeared. Then suddenly and unexpectedly, a whole branch burst out again into blossom; and it even occurred a few times that all over the movement a sea of flowers unfolded in wondrous beauty. These were the times when the ideals of Camphill were strong enough to permeate our life and work. For these flowers are the essentials of Camphill which appear, shine forth and wither away again.

Some of the flowers, however, are fertilized and change into fruits. When this occurs, we can clearly observe the results of our labour. With each fruit we make another step in the understanding of our children, of our work and our task. These fruits will never perish. They remain, endure and feed our further efforts.

The essentials of Camphill are these fruits and flowers; when they fail to unfold and grow, Camphill will not be able to develop and to keep its pledge to the handicapped child.

Today the whole civilized world is aware that even severe mental handicap can be improved under remedial education. In schools, homes and hospitals remedial education, occupational therapy and therapeutic communities are already a general rule.

The handicapped child is no longer looked upon as an imbecile person and a burden to the community. Its human abilities are recognized and great efforts are being made to treat and train, to teach and help these children.

To us, as pupils of Rudolf Steiner, the child — whatever his mental condition may be — is more than his physical appearance may indicate. He is more than his body, more than his emotions, more than his spoken or unspoken words. He is even more than his achievements. In his appearance he is merely the outer shell of an infinite and eternal spiritual being.

What does this mean? We are convinced that every human being has his individual existence not only here on earth between birth and death, but that every child was a spiritual entity before he was born, and that every man will continue to live after he has passed through the gate of death. Thus, any kind of physical or mental handicap is not acquired by chance or misfortune. It has a definite meaning for the individual and is meant to change his life.

Like any other human being who has to battle with various diseases, the handicapped child also has to learn how to live with his ailment or to conquer it. As parents and teachers, our task is to appeal to the eternal being of the child, to make him recognize his destiny. However hidden his individuality may be and however covered up by the many layers of inability, lameness and uncontrolled emotions — we must try to break through these sheaths and reach the holy of holies in every man: the seat of his spiritual entity.

The conviction that every man carries this 'I' in him and that this 'I' is eternal, imperishable and of a spiritual nature, is fundamental for our approach to the child. He is our brother and our sister. He is equal to every other human being and equal to us. We do not deal with the handicapped child; we deal with the child who is handicapped.

Many of them are retarded, paralysed, epileptic, incompetent, lazy, abnormal or backward. All this may be as it appears. The nucleus of the being, the inmost kernel of his existence is not only infinite; it is divine! It is part of the divinity to which it will return and from whence it came and will come again. His crippled and distorted life is but one among many such lives on his way back to the Father. We are all prodigal sons seeking our ways back to the house of the eternal ground of the world, the fountainhead of our existence. This is the first essential of Camphill.

And the second? Three times the Gospels relate the story of the young man who suffered from epilepsy sickness and whom the disciples could not heal. Only Christ — after having gone through the stage of Transfiguration — is able to cast out the evil spirit. And when the disciples asked him why they themselves were helpless, he replied, 'Because of your little faith. For truly, I say to you, if you have faith as a grain of mustard seed, you will say to this mountain, 'Move from here to there,' and it will move; and nothing will be impossible to you.' (Matthew 17:20)

This saying should not be taken literally but spiritually. It simply indicates that man is endowed with a power which has creative possibilities. This power can build houses and temples; it paints pictures and forms sculptures; it is the same power which invented the wheel, spanned the first bridges over a river and trained horses. This is the power which can move mountains and has done so throughout mankind's evolution.

This inner force is not man's intellect nor his intelligence. It is his ability to transform nature. It is the creative force which changes wild sceneries into lovely landscapes; the force which tills the soil and invented the potter's wheel and the weaver's loom.

This creative power is gradually fading away. Our technical civilization no longer has any place for it. The gadgets and machines do all the 'creative work' which every human being was called upon to do until the beginning of this century. This transformation is quite justified in the sphere of industrial production and everyday life. It is right to substitute central heating for an open fireplace and a washing machine for a wooden tub. It is already questionable whether a horse-drawn plough can be replaced by a tractor. And where a human being is concerned there should be no question whether machines can replace the creative ability of man. No teaching machine can be substituted for the teacher; no mechanical means for the direct contact between man and man.

The 'grain of mustard seed' of creativity is one of the fundamentals in remedial education. It has to be renewed day after day in those who work with the handicapped child. This faith 'to be able to move mountains' is the prerogative of the teacher and helper in the field of mental deficiency. He must acquire it, otherwise his work becomes stale.

Rudolf Steiner has drawn attention to this need in his lectures on curative education. He said, 'Whatever you do when treating and educating a handicapped child — you will always interfere with his destiny. It is a real interference in the child's karma.' We, as teachers and doctors, can only do the work for the retarded child if we engender in our souls the creative power which may be able to remove or at least lower the mountain of handicap.

To kindle this inner power should be the daily exercise of the teacher. He has to educate himself and to gain a steady certainty in his responsibility and conscientiousness: his responsibility for the destiny of the handicapped child; his conscientiousness for the work with his child — these are the two indispensable virtues of the curative teacher.

If the teacher and helper can achieve this, then spiritual sources are opened up and intuition will guide and replenish his labour. Every morning and evening the teacher must turn to this fountainhead of his existence; be it in prayer and meditation, or concentration and other mental exercises. Such inner education has to be pursued. Otherwise the teacher's strength will fail and his most precious gift, spiritual courage, will vanish.

As curative teachers we need undaunted energy and courage. Nothing but prayer and meditation can create this special faculty in the human soul of today. And when the disciples asked further why they were unable to cast out the evil spirit from the boy, Christ answered, 'This kind cannot be driven forth by anything but prayer and fasting.' (Mark 9:29)

Again, such words of Christ cannot be taken literally. We neither cast out spirits nor do we need to fast. 'To cast out spirits' means to create a surrounding congenial to a handicapped child. It is an environment of loving peace and peaceful love. It is a house without noise and hurry, without restlessness and quarrel. And 'to fast' means to forgo the various temptations today's life offers us: television, radio, drink, chatter, gossip and the many things that make life so difficult and unbearable. This type of everyday existence is the greatest enemy of the handicapped child.

If we are able to renounce these temptations and lead a life without that glamour, we do justice to the handicapped child by 'praying and fasting.'

Who will understand this? Today millions of cripples, disabled and impaired people are 'entertained' all over the world by the evil powers of wireless and television. With the best of intentions the worst influence is thus brought to bear. None of our houses in Camphill has television, and the radio is only turned on when special occasions make it necessary.

The inner education of the teacher is the second essential of Camphill. His endurance and sacrifice, his continued care of the child and his attempt 'to fast and pray,' thereby creating 'the grain of mustard seed' in his soul, is this second essential. We try to prepare it during our training courses. Not only knowledge is given to our students. They learn to kindle their creative forces and to make them into a continuous source of strength and sacrifice.

The third essential is the following: during the last two decades a new science has markedly moved into the foreground of common knowledge: sociology. Though it is an old science it had never been in the consciousness of the general public. But today everybody speaks about 'human relations,' 'interpersonal relationships,' 'social psychology' etc. All this is due to the growing awareness that every human being is largely dependent on his environment and under the deep and direct influence of his fellow men.

We have learned to understand the lasting influence which a mother has on her baby. We know that no infant will grow up unharmed without the loving care and personal dependence he receives from his environment. We began to recognize the powerful character formation which a family extends over its members, and we have studied the influence of the larger community on each one of its members.

In fact, we have become convinced through an overwhelming number of observations that man is — to use a word from Aristotle — a zoön politikon, a social animal. (Zoön for the Greek was more 'a living being' and not 'an animal' in today's sense and meaning.) Man is a social being! We might almost say: man can only be man when he is part of other human beings. An isolated man is unable to develop his humanity. Everyone is dependent on the other; he must communicate with the other and be recognized by the other. Every 'I' needs his 'you,' every 'me' needs his 'him' or 'her.' This is true for every human being, for the sane as much as for the insane, for the clever as for the backward. The community, whichever form it takes, is the essential womb of man.

This social womb has several layers. The innermost one is the family, the second is represented by the village or the street and district of the town. The third layer is the community of the people who speak the same language. And the outermost and largest layer is the whole of mankind. Just as no embryo can live outside the womb and its layers so no born man can live outside the womb of human community. We are born out of one womb into the other; from out of our mother's womb into the womb of society. And every infant has to adjust himself from the one environment to the other. If there is not enough loving guidance and gentle care, this adjustment will be difficult and sometimes even impossible.

Many handicapped children suffer severely under this maladjustment. The disappointment of the parents, the misunderstanding of the surroundings, the inability to interpret their strange appearance and odd behaviour drives them into isolation. This happens far more often than we realize. It is, therefore, one of the most essential conditions for remedial education and training to provide an adequate social womb with the appropriate layers of community living for handicapped children and adults. It is the basis for work with mentally afflicted people.

Since the beginning of Camphill, we were conscious of this basic need in our work. And we have never ceased to readjust our social structure and remodel it according to changing conditions.

Superficial observers and fleeting visitors often judge our way of life with a preconceived opinion. The fact that none of our co-workers receives a wage or salary is not an economic arrangement but part of our social endeavour to create the right environment for the handicapped person. We are convinced that we could not do our work in the same manner if we were employees and received a salary, because we know that work which is paid has lost its social value. No professional person can be paid for his services. As soon as it is paid, it is no longer a service! Wages (not money!) create a barrier between the one who receives and the one who pays. To give and to take is a matter of mutual human relationship; the true relationship goes as soon as wages intervene. Paid service is no service; paid love is no love; paid help has nothing to do with help.

If we begin to understand the tender connection which exists between services and social environment, a new light is shed on community for the education and care of handicapped people. This work will only succeed socially if salaries are not involved. Payments should be made in another form. They can be given as freely as the services which are rendered.

In the sphere of economy a true brotherhood must be established: a brotherhood of inequality and individual standards. Not everyone can live under similar conditions as his brother and sister. The earthly needs of men are different; yet men should learn to live in fraternity in spite of their different economic requirements.

There is, however, another social sphere where equality is necessary. This is the realm of the individual rights of people: the right to speak, to know and to do. A community of men can only function if these rights are properly observed. The realm of work — be it a school, a business, a factory or a hospital — will only be permeated by the good will of everybody if each member of this community knows the work of others or is free to inform himself about this work. He must also have the right to say how he thinks the work should be distributed, arranged and furthered. Everybody's voice must be heard. And, lastly, each co-worker must be given the opportunity to do the kind of work for which he thinks he is destined. Yet he cannot claim this right for himself without allowing the same privilege to all the others.

In the realm of human cooperation and togetherness, equality of rights, not brotherhood, is indicated. The standard of living is an individual matter; it depends on personal needs and necessities. But the difference in creative faculties, talents and working capacities call for a sphere of common rights where equal justice is done to all.

A third realm remains in the social order; it is the sphere of privacy. Neither equality nor brotherhood should permeate this social realm. It is the place where man has to be anti-social and self-contained. It is not possible in our time to be continually social. If we would do so, we would soon lose our identity and individual existence. Some sphere of privacy must be provided for each single person in a working community. Whether he wants a private room or a space for his family is his own decision. One will prefer his own workbench, the other a small library for himself, a third some time for private studies. Liberty has to rule in this social realm — but not liberty alone. The single person must also let his conscience speak so that his demands remain in harmony with the needs of the community.

If step by step these spheres of social order are achieved and adapted to the conditions of life, order and harmony will permeate the community.

Fraternity lives in the sphere of economy.
Equality is needed in the realm of cooperation.
Liberty, supported by the voice of conscience, rules
the element of privacy.

In such a community the handicapped child will feel accepted and secure; the backward and crippled adult will experience his humanity, and each co-worker can find his place to live and work creatively. This kind of social order is the third essential of Camphill.

These are the three essentials which give the basis to our life and form the background to our work. They indicate the difference between Camphill and similar schools and homes for handicapped children.

These essentials are threefold in structure and it would be difficult to establish one or even two without attempting all three together. The three essentials are interwoven with one another. Regard for the spiritual nature of one's fellow man, the endeavour of one's inner development and the establishment of a true community are a trinity; they are a threefold unity.

This threefold ideal will hardly ever find fulfilment here on earth. It should be an aim we try to achieve and a goal for which we strive; but it lies in the nature of every ideal that it can never be fully attained. This is human destiny. Nevertheless, to attempt to find the way and to walk towards an ideal are necessary.

When this is done the right atmosphere is created, which is a fundamental need for every handicapped person, child or adult. It is an atmosphere of human striving and endeavour for spiritual ideals. The handicapped personality needs an environment which is permeated by higher values, spiritual and religious.

The child in need of special care asks for the renewal of his soul. But regeneration can only occur if the child's surrounding is filled with higher values like the three essentials of Camphill. A community longing for communion with the Spirit provides the true living breath for crippled, ill and handicapped people.

The renewal of the soul by the living breath of the Spirit is the ultimate aim of remedial education. It strives for the repeated presence of the Comforter, the Holy Spirit, who is the Healing Spirit. The three essentials are one of the means to create a social condition for the Healing Spirit to work. He has the power to make every child and every man 'whole' again. But 'whole' is not 'healthy.' The Holy Spirit restores the strength to take up one's cross and to walk along the path of individual destiny.

In a community striving for the three essentials the words of John the Baptist can be heard: 'The crooked shall be made straight, and the rough ways shall be made smooth; and all flesh shall see the salvation of God.'

Since that time the provision for handicapped people has grown, improved, and in some cases, become similar to what Camphill attempts to offer today.

The wave of compassion that has swept the world since the mid-fifties has gone hand in hand with the realization that not only some are handicapped, but that today, more than ever, each human being is in need of 'the Spirit that maketh whole.'

The experience of loss of this spiritual homeland is accompanied by man's increasing dependence on the powers of technology that are advancing at a frightening pace, confronting him with an overwhelming realization of his responsibility for the planet earth today. The centres of Camphill also take part in the suffering of mankind as a whole. To be alert to the needs of the present time and to express this in deeds will require an unceasing effort from those who intend to carry the torch lit by Karl König.

1. Anke Weihs; 2. Peter Roth;
3. Marie Korach; 4. Alix Roth;
7. Trude Amann; 8. Willi Amann;
9. Alex Baum; 10. Thomas Weihs;
12. Renate König; 13. Peter Bergel;
14. Robert Linney; 15. Karl König;
16. Veronica König; 17. Andreas König;
18. Christoph König

2. The History and Development of Camphill

FRIEDWART BOCK

Camphill began in 1939–40 when a small band of young refugees from Austria, together with their mentor, Dr Karl König, found a house in the north-east of Scotland. Their new home was Camphill, a 25-acre estate seven miles from Aberdeen.

Karl König was a well-known medical practitioner who had resolved to devote his energies to the needs of the handicapped child. While practising in Vienna, a group of intellectuals and artists met in his study group — they studied Rudolf Steiner's anthroposophy — and set their sights on establishing a community for handicapped people. The political oppression in Austria and Germany in 1938 made them apply in turn to France, Cyprus, Ireland and Britain. Just before the outbreak of the Second World War, Britain opened its doors to them. Dr König arrived in London late in 1938 and wrote to his young friends on December 19:

> Yesterday I returned from Scotland where Mr and Mrs Haughton had invited me to tell them of our plans. In their estate near Insch, Aberdeenshire, there is a vacant manse which they would like to acquire for our use. It would be suitable, to begin with, to accommodate us and fifteen to twenty children. During the first months we will be supplied with food. Dear friends, this Christmas we will permeate our hearts with good will for our work which shall become the working of the World Word.

We are permitted to look back with gratitude upon a destiny which has guided us with so much blessing. We look forward with joy to the work we want to accomplish.

One by one the group from Europe arrived at Kirkton House. Although there was no electricity or heating they had made a home there. Children with special needs were taken in, and on May 28, 1939, the opening ceremony was performed in the small rectory overlooking the granite hills north of the River Don. The war began and following Dunkirk the group was classified as 'enemy aliens' and the men interned.

A larger house was found, Camphill House on the Royal Deeside, and purchased by the publisher Mr WF Macmillan. It was let to Camphill at a nominal rental and all loans were repaid in 1943. In the absence of the men, the move was accomplished by the women, chiefly Tilla König, Alix Roth and Anke Weihs, and on June 1, 1940, the life and work of Camphill began. Later in the year the men returned from internment on the Isle of Man to find Camphill well established, and about twelve children in residence. In an interview with the Aberdeen Press and Journal on October 21, 1940, Dr König said:

Kirkton House near Insch, Aberdeenshire

Camphill House from the west

I have several English and refugee children here at present, but I hope to do something for Scottish children especially. I was told by the Board of Control in Edinburgh that this is the first private institution for such children in this country. In addition to twenty-four children we will be able to care for adults at a lodge and cottage on the estate. The children become part of a community under our system — and it is of course, a Christian community.

Standing: Willi Amann, Peter Roth, Anke Weihs, Thomas Weihs, Alex Baum, Tilla König. Sitting: Trude Amann, Marie Korach, Alix Roth

Tilla König

Alix Roth

Profiles of some members of the founding group

Tilla König was born in 1902 in Silesia, Germany, and had a Moravian Brethren upbringing. Her work with children led her to Arlesheim, Switzerland, where she met Karl König. Both studied with Ita Wegman. After their marriage in 1929 the Königs built up a curative educational home in Pilgramshain, Silesia, before moving to Vienna, and from there to Kirkton House, Aberdeenshire, as refugees. They established Camphill in 1940. Tilla's attitude to each person and each thing was an example for all who worked with her. She died in 1983 at Camphill Alpha, South Africa.

Alix Roth was born in 1916 in Vienna where she worked as a photographer. She was introduced to anthroposophy in the youth group at Dr König's house, together with her brother and his friends. In Camphill she was at the centre of the nurses' work and vital in founding the work in Central Europe. She died in 1987 at Aigues Vertes, Geneva.

Anke Weihs was born in 1914 in Melbourne, Australia. She went to Vienna in 1930 as a dancer. After meeting the youth group gathered around Dr König, she joined those who went to Scotland as refugees. Her contribution was outstanding by virtue of its creativity. She died in 1987 at Camphill Aberdeen.

Anke Weihs

Trude Amann was born in 1915 in Vienna where she met the founding group before training in curative education at Arlesheim, Switzerland. What she learned there remained a source of inspiration for the therapeutic work to come. She died in 1987 at Camphill Aberdeen.

Barbara Lipsker was the first of the group who met Karl König when she looked after his two older children in Vienna. She became a member of the youth group and escaped to England, working as an au pair. She joined the group at Camphill House at Christmas 1940. She was for many years the principal at Glencraig, Northern Ireland.

Marie Korach came in contact with Alix and Peter Roth at an early age. She joined the group of founders in Kirkton House at Whitsun, 1939.

Trude Amann

Thoman Weihs

Thomas Weihs was born in 1914 in Vienna, where he studied medicine and met the youth group together with his friend Peter Roth. After graduating in Basel he came to Britain on the last boat before the war and joined the little community in Kirkton House. He worked in agriculture and eventually took over the medical curative work from Dr König. He died in 1983 at Camphill Aberdeen.

Carlo Pietzner

Carlo Pietzner was born in 1915 in Vienna. He became a member of the youth group while training as an artist and joined the small community after its move to Camphill House in 1941. He was central in the founding of the work in Glencraig, Northern Ireland, and from 1960, in the United States. He died in 1986 at Copake, New York.

Alex Baum

Alex Baum was born in 1910 in Vienna. He was one of the first to join the youth group around Dr König in 1936. He studied chemistry but had to flee to Britain to escape Nazi oppression and linked up with the other founders at Kirkton House in 1939. The teaching impulse and the furthering of eurythmy were his particular concerns. He died in Munich in 1975.

Peter Roth began his medical studies at eighteen and found his way to Dr König's youth group. Later he became a priest of the Christian Community and pioneered the Camphill village work at Botton, England, where he is an influence to this day.

Hans and Lisl Schauder, and Willi Amann were also members of the founding group, first in Vienna and then in the north-east of Scotland. They left in 1943 to start Garvald in Peeblesshire, south of Edinburgh.

Newton Dee farmhouse from the south-west

Newton Dee farmhouse from the south-east

Cairnlee House from the west

Heathcote House, Aberdeenshire

Murtle House, Aberdeenshire

*Birthday celebration at
Heathcote House with Tilla König*

Seven decades of Camphill

So the first decade began. The preliminary development at Kirkton House was now set to grow and develop at Camphill. At a time when the War escalated in Europe, North Africa and Asia, the plight of the children in need of special care was brought to Karl König and his friends. The small community at Camphill thrived. In 1942 Heathcot House on the south side of the river was rented to cope with the constant need for further places. In these early years most of the children were sent privately to Camphill.

In April 1944, Murtle House was acquired with its 35 acres. With three separate properties there would be no pressure on numbers; but then a group of lads who had been before the juvenile courts and presented various degrees of delinquency came to Camphill. They benefited directly from the presence of the more frail and handicapped children, but Camphill did not have the facilities to give them what they needed. In March 1945, Newton Dee, an estate of 170 acres, came on the market, and was acquired with the help of Helen Macmillan, who was later repaid. The farm and workshops at Newton Dee provided ideal facilities for the lads.

Thomas Weihs on Newton Dee Farm

St John's play at Murtle, 1952, with view of the Dee Valley (left), and Murtle House after the play (right)

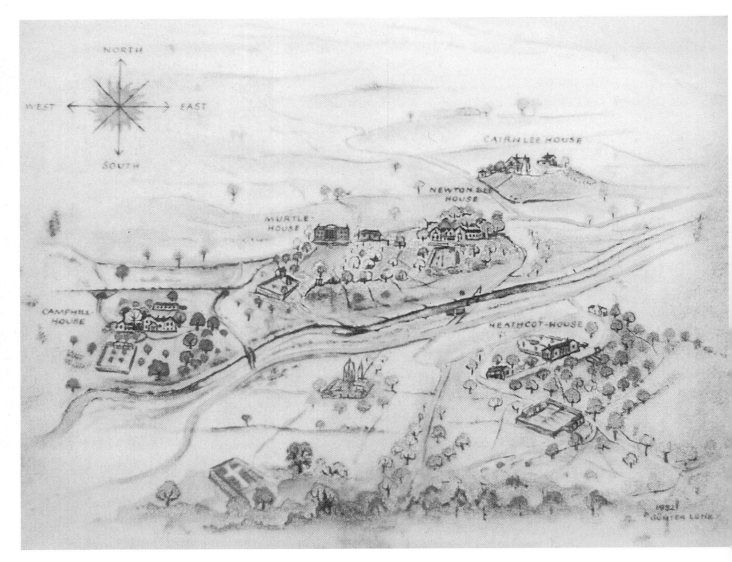

Picture map of Camphill, Murtle, Newton Dee, Cairnlee and Heathcote

In 1947–48, St John's School, a small Waldorf school for co-workers' children and local children from Aberdeen, opened at Murtle. Three years later all pupils and staff children were included in this schooling because Karl König recognized the potential benefit of Waldorf teaching for all children.

Just before the end of the foundation decade, Camphill featured in an article in an illustrated weekly, the *Picture Post*. In the April 30, 1949 issue, Fyfe Robertson wrote:

> Individual treatment is the chief secret of Camphill's successes. The basic treatment for all is good, naturally-grown, balanced food; intelligent medical care; a serene and regular life, and above all, the affection which these children need and which can sometimes make them flower wonderfully.
>
> Of the 180 children at these schools, about 100 are unable to use speech properly, and hardly any of the children can move harmoniously and gracefully. Both conditions are concerned with voluntary muscle control, and Camphill uses the Steiner method to deal with this. Music, colour and 'curative eurythmy' — in which the children are taught, by special alphabet movements of the limbs, to 'speak' with the whole body — are bringing results. If one can loosen the speech organs, the main battle is won — and the locked personality will be partly freed. It really should not surprise us that speech, which has been so powerful in emancipating and bemusing the mind of man, acts in this way as an integrator of the personality.

The *Picture Post* article included many photographs and brought a spate of inquiries. A waiting list for children had to be set up.

In October 1949, a Camphill Seminar course began for young people who wanted to learn about curative education. Many hundreds have completed the Camphill Seminar in the twelve centres where the course is now conducted. The seminar has a seminal quality and has been vital to the growth of the movement.

The second decade, from 1950 to 1959, began with the acquisition of the fifth estate, Cairnlee, initially for the use of severely disturbed adolescent girls. Age groups were segregated

The Sheiling, Ringwood, England

Thornbury House, Bristol, England

Thornbury Park, Bristol, England

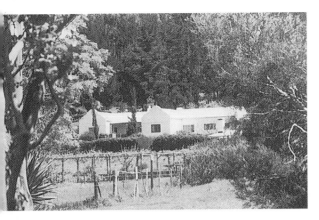

Dawn Farm, Hermanus, South Africa

Downingtown, Pennsylvania, USA

Below: The Lehenhof, Lake Constance, Germany

into different houses and estates right up to 1964, after which a wide spectrum of ages was placed in every house.

There were now 240 children, with a roughly equal number of private and local authority referrals, but local authority referrals were soon to outstrip the private ones. Karl König strongly maintained the educability of every child, however handicapped. Legislation caught up with this view only very gradually, beginning in 1959, and established the principle of education for *all* children in 1974.

The main feature of Camphill's second decade was the move into England, Ireland, South Africa, Germany and the United States. Mrs Redman of South Africa had seen the *Picture Post* article and asked Dr König to help in her country. In 1951 a Camphill-trained teacher went out to Dawn Farm, Hermanus. Calls from individual parents or parents' associations were met by Camphill opening centres in England at the Sheiling, Ringwood and Thornbury, Bristol, in 1951, and at Glencraig in Northern Ireland in 1953. The step to continental Europe was made when work with children suffering from spasticity was established at Brachenreuthe, Germany, in 1958, following a similar call. In 1959 Camphill was asked to take over an existing small curative home in Downingtown, Pennsylvania, from an elderly couple, and this led to the rapid growth of the work in the United States during the sixties. During the same year Christophorus, Holland, a small home school established six years earlier, joined the Camphill family. During this phase the Camphill Movement, a network of identity embracing all the Camphill centres, was born.

Karl König and Alix Roth at the opening of Camphill Hall, September 22, 1962

A significant diversification of the Camphill work took place in 1954 with the establishment of the first village for handicapped adults in Botton on the Yorkshire moors. Again it was parents who prompted this development by their insistence that Camphill could do this. The base for village work had been created at Newton Dee as early as 1945. In 1952 Karl König wrote in a report:

> I would wish that in later years Camphill might become a place where the conscience for curative education will be kept awake — a place where the true destiny of the handicapped child will always be known ... It should always grow into a place where those children, not attaining sufficient improvements to go out into the world, could remain and have a sheltered yet useful life. They could do some limited work in the various kitchens and workshops, the houses, the farm and the gardens. They should not live in dormitories but in small houses in the lap of the family to which they belong and where they feel safe and secure. Thus around each one of our houses a very small village should grow with four or five small houses occupied by a few families finding their place in life and work. The idea of a true village community, growing ever deeper, will have to find roots in our efforts.

Brachenreuthe, Germany, looking towards Lake Constance

Below: Whitsun pageant at Camphill Hall

Below: The opening of Föhrenbühl, Lake Constance, Germany, 1963

Barbara Lipsker, Anke Weihs, Peter Roth, Kate Roth and Thomas Weihs at Camphill, September 1962

Botton Hall, Yorkshire

Glencraig, Northern Ireland

His vision became reality two years later. It is a remarkable stroke of destiny that the Botton property which was selected for the first village was the Macmillan family's former country estate.

The destiny of a movement is bound up with that of its founder. Camphill's second decade saw Dr König's serious illness in 1955 and his decision in 1957 to pass on his duties as superintendent of the Camphill Rudolf Steiner Schools to Thomas Weihs, while he remained as consultant. Dr König also took up the task of chairman of the Camphill Movement. As an organ of the Camphill Movement the *Cresset* was launched, a quarterly journal that appeared for eighteen years. One part of the *Cresset's* aims was that:

> The *Cresset* shall be an expression of the Camphill Movement's innermost urge to help carry forward the glow brought to life by Rudolf Steiner to the end that the contemporary knowledge of man be enflamed by the fire of love.

The third decade (1960–69) began with Newton Dee's change of task: moving from a school setting for adolescent handicapped boys to become the second major village for adults. The following year, in 1961, a village was established near Geneva, Switzerland.

The nodal point in this middle decade was the laying of the foundation stone of the Camphill Hall on July 1, 1961. This year also marked the centenary of Rudolf Steiner's birth and the 21st anniversary of the founding of Camphill. The building of the hall became the expression of the concerted efforts of the movement to build a space where conferences could be held; where the work could be developed and deepened. The opening of the Camphill Hall in September 1962 was at the same time a tribute by the movement to its founder whose sixtieth birthday fell in that month.

Two years later, in 1964, Dr König relinquished his place as chairman of the Camphill Movement, a truly exemplary move, having divided the movement into six regions, each with its own chairman. He moved back to Germany to strengthen the work there and to chair a region comprising the centres around Lake Constance and Lake Geneva. Thus the Camphill Movement was regionalized and the administration decentralized. Camphill Aberdeen was no longer the centre of the movement, yet it has long remained a focal point.

The work in Germany made great strides during 1964 when Föhrenbühl opened its doors for many children as a neighbour to Brachenreuthe. The following September, the first German village, at the Lehenhof, was opened by Dr König.

When Karl König died in March 1966, he had seen his vision of a community with the handicapped person come to reality. He had seen the expansion of the movement from its central position, and then to the development of a decentralized but interrelating autonomy, which is a true deed of brotherliness.

In 1966 a village was founded at Vidaråsen, Norway, following a first unsuccessful attempt twelve years earlier. Now Camphill had a Scandinavian region, which has seen a string of villages develop in subsequent years.

Glencraig, Northern Ireland

St John's festival

Donald Perkins (with beret) at Camphill

King Arthur pageant, Whitsun 1979

Hall with Murtle House, from the south

Hans Heinrich Engel was active as a physician in Scotland and Northern Ireland for many years before his untimely death in 1973

The fourth ten-year period, the seventies, began with the Sylvia-Koti School in Finland joining the Camphill Movement in 1970, making it the easternmost centre, and the one closest to Russia. Through the personal initiative of a couple from the Ringwood centre, a small Camphill school was established in Botswana in 1974: Camphill Rankoromane.

The seventies saw growth in the work with adolescents and young adults: Coleg Elidyr in Wales, Templehill, Blair Drummond, Corbenic and Beannachar in Scotland, together with a school at Ochil Tower. In 1976 a village was established at Liebensfels, Austria, 38 years after Karl König and his young friends had to leave their homeland to found and establish the work in Scotland.

Thomas Weihs's book *Children in Need of Special Care* was published in 1971, and remains a popular book for parents, students, teachers and specialists. It expresses Camphill's therapeutic principles and has gone through editions in Britain and America, as well as being translated into Spanish, Portuguese, Italian, German, French and Japanese. In 1975 *Camphill Correspondence* was first published as the second Camphill journal.

The Camphill Eurythmy School began at Ringwood in 1970, and later also in Botton. The eurythmy training is fully integrated into the life of both centres, and many talented young people are trained for artistic and therapeutic work within and outside Camphill.

In 1979 Camphill became a full member of the Konferenz for Curative Education and Social Therapy at Dornach, Switzerland. This body embraces all the work done in this field in the name of Rudolf Steiner.

A Camphill village started in Le Béal, France, in May 1979. The French authorities accepted the Camphill Seminar certificate as equivalent to the diploma in special education. Another Camphill village began in Angaia, Brazil, during the same year.

In the eighties further diversification took place, including work with the elderly and with care units in the villages. Growth of urban communities was characteristic of the eighties. In England local authorities invited Camphill to develop a centre within the town perimeter at Milton Keynes and in Middlesborough.

A further village started at Sauk Centre, Minnesota, in 1980. In Sweden, Staffansgården, a village which had existed for nine years became a Camphill village in 1983. In Scotland, Loch Arthur village began near Dumfries in 1984. In 1988 the first community for young adults, Soltane, was acquired in America. This development signalled a new step for the region.

An increase in government regulations relating to the care of the handicapped took place during the decade. These addressed questions of staff qualifications, registration of centres and led to restrictions on co-workers from abroad working in Camphill centres. National associations were formed throughout the movement to act for the centres, and the advice and help of external council members and directors is increasingly required.

While Camphill extended its work worldwide, the circle of supporters also grew. A first international meeting of Camphill board (council) members took place at Ringwood in 1987 with eighty delegates and a further meeting took place in the anniversary year at Camphill Aberdeen.

The 1980s were a period when several of the founder group of Camphill pioneers died, all well into their seventies. Thomas Weihs died in 1983, Carlo Pietzner in 1986, Trude Amann, Alix Roth and Anke Weihs in 1987. They left a wide field of tasks to the coming generations.

Public honours were awarded to several friends for their, and Camphill's, contribution to work with the handicapped. In Germany Karl König received the Tutzing Star on October 27, 1963, and Ursula Herberg the BVK; in Britain, Peter Roth received an OBE, and Barbara Lipsker, Ann Harris and Lotte Sahlmann MBEs.

The Camphill Movement with its 72 centres was then grouped into seven regions: Scotland, England and Wales, Ireland, Scandinavia, Central Europe, North America and Southern Africa.

The phase of the 'founders' or 'pioneers' was followed by the group of 'followers' and then the 'successors.' All of these were torch-bearers of the impulse to build communities with the disabled.

The fiftieth anniversary of Camphill in 1990 was marked by films and the publication of *A Candle on the Hill* and the *Camphill Dialogue*. Many members of the founder group had died already, but Peter Roth was still active until his death in 1997. A very few lived longer and made the step into the 21st Century. Barbara Lipsker and Marie Korach lived to experience the centenary of Karl König in 2002. Hans Schauder, who had moved out of Camphill, died in Edinburgh in 2001. In January 1992 Hans wrote:

We have received *A Candle on the Hill* and thank you
most warmly for this magnificent present. It is indeed
a great and glorious book and in every way a working
witness to the scope and the power of the Camphill
Movement. Indeed, looking at it from time to time,
we feel that *A Candle on the Hill* is far too modest a
title. It comes across to us rather as 'a shining light
on many hills.'

Thank you again,
Hans and Lisl Schauder

In September 2001 I had a conversation with Barbara Lipsker
in Glencraig. She said:

I can look back on my life, I can only say thank
you, I was graced to be guided. I still wonder how
much the human life can encompass. I have so many
friends, I felt so connected to your group, Jens,
Gerda, Taco, Udo, Christof Andreas, Karin — a
special time.

Marie Korach outlived all the other pioneers; she died in
October 2002. The following words were written by Gunther
Lehr:

Now you as well
Have entered the land of Truth and Life
The last link in the golden chain
has softly left behind all earthly matter
to close the ring of friends in Spirit's Land
who have decided soon to turn their longing to the Earth
prepared to give again
their light-filled self
into the dark ground
with helping will of sacrifice,
that suffering may be healed —
enkindling hearts again
and founding brotherhood of peace.

During the twenty years between 1990 and 2010 the work
of Camphill has expanded worldwide, while a couple of earlier
foundations had to revise their work and take a step back.

While hearing of new beginnings in Hungary and Vietnam, the contributions made by Angaia, Brazil and Templehill were no longer viable. The overall movement is looking towards the future to ensure the regions of the Camphill Movement are able to respond to needs, and that calls for help can be met. Young people have trained in Camphill and carry their experience and insight into the world like emissaries. Older people in Camphill seek to renew the impulse and to rekindle the flame where it may have grown dim.

It is quite a challenge to extend one's awareness and interest to the many centres of the Camphill Movement and to the colleagues who work there, but the endeavour to do so benefits the whole and strengthens the cooperation. Every co-worker in Camphill is capable of experiencing any change within the body of Camphill. This awareness and perception is instrumental in the worldwide community building.

Listening to the karma of both children and adults requires a tactful sensitivity. This perception is also directed to the development of the work in general and will be needed even more in future years.

The original impulse of Camphill was to build communities together with those in need of special understanding. Some centres may appear forgetful of this with employment of co-workers and satellite living. Notwithstanding, there is always the readiness to answer a call for help and meet the needs of our time.

The need for qualifications is formidable in the face of regulations introduced relentlessly by the state. Our answer to this lies hopefully in the courses developed by ourselves in conjunction with academic institutions. The Bachelor of Arts in Curative Education, now being renamed Social Pedagogy, at Aberdeen is just one such example.

We are often asked if our work in Camphill is developing further. Our work diversifies due to the abundance of challenging tasks we face when working with children, youngsters and adults. Significant developments have taken place in a number of schools and village communities. The programme designed for the training of the young adults with special needs is very fruitful. It includes work experience, learning skills in crafts and land work as well as courses taken at the local college. The range of therapies on offer is beneficial: therapeutic eurythmy, music and art therapy, speech and play therapy, riding, counselling and physiotherapy. In the course of time the villages have become an integral part of their locality.

Books written by Camphill people are a growing manifestation of how curative education and social therapy are presented. At the time of writing, the important book by Thomas Weihs, *Children in Need of Special Care*, had once again been reprinted; it has continued to offer essential help to professionals and parents alike since it first appeared in 1971. Karl König's *Village Lectures* appeared in a new revised edition, *Seeds of Social Renewal*, in 2009. Other new titles include *Holistic Special Education*, edited by Robin Jackson (2006), *Living Buildings* by Joan de Ris Allen (1990), *Karl König, a Middle-European Destiny* by Hans Müller-Wiedemann (1992), *The Builders of Camphill*, edited by Friedwart Bock (2004), *The Lives of Camphill*, edited by Johannes Surkamp (2007). Others to note are *Autism, a Holistic Approach* by B Woodward and M Hogenboom and *Growing Eco Communities* by J Bang (2009). You will find full details of all of these as well as many others in the bibliography (page 241). Numerous essays and research papers have appeared in journals, both in German and English. The dissertations of the students of the BA in Curative Education, the Youth Guidance Seminar, the Adult Communities' course and the Kate Roth Seminar have the potential to offer the results of research into our anthroposophical sources and in current trends.

Much progress has been made in the legal, administrative field. The first Camphill Dialogue in 1987 in Ringwood was followed every three years by another one, to enable the board members of the international Camphill Movement to meet. Some centres find it necessary to employ managers who may at first have little insight in the socio-economic side of the work, but who often rise quickly and helpfully to their new task. The threefold social order (see Chapter 3 article by Michael Luxford for a fuller description of the threefold social order) continues to inspire our work as we endeavour to realise the Three Essentials in our communities.

Research, study, learning
Celebrating the Christian festivals
The basic social law in the economic field

When reflecting on the past seventy years, we come to the early beginnings and the forces that were at work then.

A special tribute is due to Karl König and the group of young pioneers who built the first community with children who have special needs. Their work has grown and diversified and constitutes the entire Camphill Movement today. The very fact that the British government made this beginning possible in a time of threatening war and persecution is a cause for gratitude. In retrospect, many miracles have occurred and would appear as an intrinsic part of the growth of Camphill. To recall just one of these: in Karl König's essay, 'A Candle on the Hill', of summer 1961, we learn that the application to Ireland was unsuccessful. Maybe this was due to an element of anti-semitism? An application to Cyprus was considered, not knowing that the Commonwealth instructions for the UK Delegation to the Evian Conference on Emigration from Germany of July 6, 1938, listed Cyprus as offering: no prospects, except a few butchers with capital above five hundred pounds. Karl König's application would clearly have been turned down. France had also been considered, maybe rather unwisely, at a time of impending military conflict. Ita Wegman's question, 'Why do you not try Scotland?' pointed the way forward and the letter from the British Consulate in Berne opened the doors for the group. Both Eugen Kolisko and Cecil Harwood had helped behind the scenes.

A professional advisor from Scotland wrote recently, 'Communities such as Camphill that dare to be different in rooting what they do within a particular set of values can hold a mirror to much of residential care in Scotland.'

If this refers to the work in Scotland it may be equally applicable to other countries where Camphill is now actively engaged. Let's hope that many others will take the impulse of Camphill into the future.

3. Aspects of Camphill

Camphill and anthroposophy

CORNELIUS PIETZNER

Thinking of the deep connection between Camphill and anthroposophy, out of which it grew, orientates one towards the early beginnings of Camphill and brings to mind three aspects: the original intentions and purposes behind the founding motivations of Camphill; what has developed since those beginnings and its compatibility with the original imaginations, and, thirdly, it gives strength and resolve either to continue in those directions even if they are at variance with the original intentions, or it provides correctives, if needed, regarding directions for the future. As with the lives of all complex organisms, development and growth occurs in a non-linear or multi-dimensional manner that is less predictable than one might expect. This is probably to the good.

An important opportunity lies in coming close to, even submerging oneself in, the collection of forces that flow into a larger stream, and are fundamental to and carry the ongoing work of Camphill. This 'energetic' stream is a very particular one in regard to Camphill. It is a confluence of many smaller rivulets and impulses. And although Camphill reflects a cosmopolitan orientation and an increasingly diverse activity, geography and organization, it is ultimately connected to a specific, common and formative force. One can call this spiritual identity. This identity or spiritual force flows into a group of people as intention and motivation, pictures and images, attitudes and striving, and is consciously nurtured by these groups of people. These forces are also 'offered' back having been 'individualized' and worked through by common human endeavour. This is a circular process which connects the individual to a group, which itself wishes to connect to archetypal, spiritual imaginations, pictures and impulses that motivate and provide inspiration for the daily ongoing tasks. These are the tasks of Camphill life and this process is a community-building initiative. It draws its substance and content from anthroposophical spiritual science. It is a unique mixture of inner content, individual striving, community purpose and civil engagement ideals, which blend in to each other to form the unique alchemy of spiritual community building and social renewal work that one knows as Camphill.

I have the image that the different elements of this alchemy combine and weave the many and diverse strands and threads together in a colourful and luminous braid stretching invisibly around the earth. This invisible braid connects Camphill initiatives and Camphill co-workers the world over. At times it can become thin and weak, needing refreshment both in individuals and in communities that it touches. And at other times or for specific occasions, events or locations it strengthens and pulses with a palpable emanation.

The concentration of this spiritual identity and its translation and expression into soul and physical landscapes allows an individual like Sir Laurens van der Post (whom I asked to write the Introduction to *Candle on the Hill* twenty years ago) to remark:

> I have no doubt that Camphill is an expression of a
> great intuitive thrust out of the deep heart of nature
> which has us in its keeping, and knows that both we
> and it are in mortal peril ...

This intuitive thrust out of the deep heart of nature can alternatively be seen as a concentrate of the deep spiritual forces that flow together to create a community oriented to the healing and protection of the individual in need of special soul care, and to the land through building living communities.

Van der Post could feel this and thereby perceive something of the spirit of Camphill, not only in the external expression of a piece of land (in this case Botswana), but in what Claus Otto Scharmer once described to me as 'the quality of place.' This has to do with the impregnation of a life force into a location, directed by a cultivated consciousness that is consistent, focussed and caring. This represents a devoted attention to the details of an environment that includes soil and soul, house and heart, farm and friendship, and so on. It is also a reflection of what binds and connects Camphill and its people — in short, the spirit of Camphill.

Another aspect of the interlinking of Camphill's mission with anthroposophy includes five core areas that are practised and acknowledged as essential to the work and community ethic of Camphill. They include: the element of personal transformation, meditative practice and personal development — that is, the willingness to become someone different through active inner schooling and the ordering of one's personal soul life. This ushers us directly into the world of metamorphosis and development.

The second is connected to (re)creating an archetypal picture or image of the human being as a soul-spiritual entity. The active imagination we hold — our mobile and living picture of the Image of the Human Being bearing a spirit entelechy transcendent of the physical body — translates directly into a broader ethic of daily work with other human beings, many of whom are individuals with some sort of disability. The first element gives validity and fullness to the experience of the second. The imagination and living picture of each individual having an intact, pure higher 'I' that struggles to work into, with and through the soul and body constitutes not only a 'study of humankind' but provides a foundation for respect and appreciation of all human beings.

The third area is concerned with the invisible dimensions of community building — the inner contours, practices, methods and experiences that relate to the formation and perception of social life, of life amongst ourselves, so to speak. It relates to emotional intelligence and social capacity as modalities of perception and activity in social engagement. Knowing extends beyond conventional cognitive intelligence. A knowing of the heart that comes into creative expression within a community of individuals indicates what Rudolf Steiner referred to as the transformation of the Royal Art of ancient temple building into the new Social Art. Temples of the future are to be built out of mutual brotherly/sisterly recognition and acknowledgment, a social soul temple built with the new 'bricks and mortar' of knowledge and truth, of aesthetics and beauty, and responsibility and strength.

The fourth area traces the lemniscate of human incarnation and excarnation as part of the mystery of human destiny and individual karma. It connects the external dimensions of life's occurrences with the dramatic inner aspect of biography. Both aspects belong intimately together and influence each other. This element embraces the question of purpose and meaning through reincarnation and the experience of a higher 'self' having a core purpose in life. It includes the difficulties and wonders of an individual destiny unfolding in all its chaos and precision.

The fifth area is related to our orientation in the realm of supersensible entities, from the forces that work in the elements of earth, water, air and warmth, to the ranks of Hierarchies and to the Cosmic Sun Being, present in the life-sphere surrounding the earth. It has to do with the relationship we cultivate to the guiding Spirit of our Time, Michael, and the ongoing attempt to connect our individual and community goals to humankind's goal. In other words, can we elevate what we do, in all simplicity and modesty, to something that serves humankind? This is perhaps more an inner gesture of consciousness in which one orientates and connects daily work and simple tasks to the needs of humankind. This is a 'grounding' element regarding spiritual orientation.

Alix Roth, one of the founders of Camphill, once stated in a conversation that ultimately Camphill was a 'peace mission!' This both surprised me and resounded deeply and lastingly. It helped me better understand the broader context and some of the important thoughts and images connected to the spirit of Camphill, such as Christian Rosenkreutz, the Angel of the Buddha, St John, Iphigenia, Caspar Hauser and other figures belonging to this alchemy of Camphill. These personalities, and the qualities and events they represent, help build the luminous braid embracing the world of Camphill. Studying them and their complementary mission creates a gateway into the spiritual and social mission of Camphill. Indeed, coming close to them allows us to enter the crucial stream of original intentions and purpose that formed the beginnings of Camphill and will carry it into the future.

The threefold social order

MICHAEL LUXFORD

Rudolf Steiner was occupied for at least 25 years with the attempt to deepen his understanding of how the human being is constituted from a threefold point of view. In 1899 he wrote an essay on Goethe's fairy tale *The Green Snake and the Beautiful Lily* (Steiner, *The Character of Geothe's Spirit*), in which he said:

> In the human being who is on the way to free personality, three powers of the soul are mixed together: will (bronze), feeling (silver) and knowledge (gold). Experience in life provides, through its revelation, that the soul can acquire three powers: *strength*, through which virtue can work, is revealed in the will: *beauty* is revealed in the feeling: *wisdom* reveals itself in knowledge. What separates man from 'free personality' is that these three work in his soul as a mixture as represented by the figure of the mixed or fourth king. The human being will only achieve free personality in the measure to which he can receive in full consciousness the gifts of these three with their own special quality, each of them separately, and uniting them within himself, through a free and conscious activity within himself. Only then what has previously enslaved him collapses into itself as a chaotic mixture of will, feeling and power of knowledge.

It took him until 1916 to recognize a link between the three powers and attributes of the soul, which he had written about in 1899, to the human physical organism. In a lecture in *Riddles of the Soul* he points to the relationship of human *thinking* to the nerve system, of *feeling* to the rhythmic system, and of *will activity* to the limbs and metabolic system.

Through a process of spiritual research he had recognized an archetypal threefold principle to be present in human life, both in soul and physical manifestations. This research process led him from the above consolidation of perception to a new level of insight, as is manifest in the publication of *Towards Social Renewal* in 1919. Here he speaks of a threefoldness or tripartite configuration within social life. The ideals of the French Revolution: freedom, equality, brotherhood, can be seen to be the social goals for which humanity as a whole can aspire in its cultural life, in the realm of human rights, and in economic activity, respectively. In this process Steiner gradually built a bridge of understanding between the spheres of social life, the human soul, the physical constitution and ultimately the realm of the Trinity.

Towards Social Renewal unveils a threefold dimension to the social organism, just as much as *Riddles of the Soul* opens up perspectives on the human soul in relation to our physiological constitution. However, it is now understood that these two realms need no longer remain separate, as the human individual is seen to be inextricably linked to the social organism of which he cannot help but be a part.

Anyone can become a student of the subject of threefoldness and the threefold social order. Study and interest in such matters is available to every human being as part of his or her own spiritual life. *Towards Social Renewal* is a basic book. Karl König's *Man as a Social Being and the Mission of Conscience* is also worth reading, as is *Shaping Globalization* by Nicanor Perlas. The latter book is a contemporary analysis of the problem of globalisation, and describes how the concept of threefoldness has been introduced into the governance of a modern state, in this case, the Philippines.

The following edited words of Rudolf Steiner summarise in a succinct form the ethos of each of the three dimensions of social life.

> *Spiritual life*: creativity and freedom. What flourishes at any given time, springs from what the inner productive powers of individuals can bring into life. These are the powers that develop freely in individual souls.

In Camphill this has traditionally manifested itself in the College Meeting. The holding of College Meetings is not unique to the Camphill Movement. They have their origin in the Rudolf Steiner Waldorf schools. Nonetheless, they have played a significant role in creating a Camphill 'way of life' in as far as they have been used over many decades as a specific method for attempting to understand further the needs of individuals, and to address community questions. It is also the area which promotes learning, education, cultural life and research.

> *Human rights*: inclusion and equality. The content of majority resolutions is democratic only if every single individual is on an equal basis with every other individual. They can only be adopted when everyone involved is considered an adult, and is therefore capable of judging.

In Camphill this approach is encapsulated in practising the Bible Evening, whose origin lies in an inspirational experience of Karl König's. Such a practice can lead to the emergence of new perspectives in the spheres of human relationships, community life and on the life of Christ. After Bible Evenings houses have often felt 'different,' better, or found that something of an intangible nature had occurred.

> *Economic life*: obligation and connectedness. We need to achieve the integrating of our own selves into the community in a real way. We can achieve this when the other person's need becomes part of my own inner experience. Then I will be able to respond to them out of a feeling of general connectedness. If such experiences are cultivated, then we will be called upon to contribute and work together to create a healthy social organism, and not merely for our own benefit. This can happen no matter how seemingly small or large each one's capacities might be at first sight.

The area of working life is focussed upon particularly in Rudolf Steiner's *The Social Principle, or Fundamental Social Law*:

> In a community of human beings working together, the well-being of the community will be the greater, the less the individual claims for himself the proceeds of the work he has himself done; i.e. the more of these proceeds he makes over to his fellow workers, and the more his own requirements are satisfied, not out of his own work, but out of the work done by others.

In places where The Social Principle in its different aspects is the 'modus operandi,' it may be that through its operating presence 'the well-being of the community' will be enhanced, over the course of time. The ability of Camphill communities to develop as they have done, and to expend such amounts of capital on the basis of surpluses despite having low incomes, is an indicator of such well-being. Attitudes towards work, care for the environment and fellow community members, attention to detail and the like, can give rise to an 'intangible sensing' of health.

Thus, the College Meeting and its realm is an expression of an active free spiritual life. The Bible Evening and its extended sphere of influence represents a longing for the establishing of equality, human rights and human dignity. The Social Principle seeks to promote, in practical terms, a genuinely fraternal, productive and cooperative way of life.

To have discovered these three avenues of practice and methodology, and to have placed them side by side as a working concept, is a unique achievement. However, it is the case that what was once 'a given' is now under scrutiny! In each of these three spheres of activity changes have been underway for quite some time, and in some cases earlier practices have been given up. What will be the outcome of these changes for the Camphill Movement? Are other coherent proposals available to our communities, when the demand for accountability, transparency and value-for-money tend to change social enterprises? The answer to this question is a challenge for the Camphill Movement, and in my view describing and practising the core features of the threefold social order in a modern context is the starting point.

It needs to be said that Karl König's idea was not to 'institute' a threefold social order endeavour. He saw threefoldness as inherent in natural processes, in the human being, as well as in the social order, and therefore:

> These three spheres are always within us and around
> us. The idea of the threefold social order was not
> intended *to determine* the three spheres, but rather
> to be the means by which to divide and distinguish
> them.
> (König, *Man as a Social Being*)

And:

> What we can do is not to preach the threefold social
> order, but, in a humble way, to learn to understand it.
> (König, *Man as a Social Being*)

As much as we find elements of the three dimensions of social life present in the three pillars of the Camphill Movement, and in the various writings of Karl König, such as *The Three Essentials of Camphill* (The Cresset, Michaelmas 1965), it has to be acknowledged that the above mentioned Social Principle is of particular importance for the Camphill Movement. One could ask, 'What is the relationship between the threefold social order and The Social Principle, with the latter's impulse to create healthy communities?'

My view is that the expression of this relationship is found in Camphill, for example: in adult education and the self-reflection of individuals; in working with delegation of responsibility; and in forming social funds.

It seems to be the case that threefoldness and The Social Principle unite where:

1) There is work on self-development and the attempt to overcome negative tendencies in order to benefit the community.
2) Where there is the wish to hold inclusive discussions, delegate responsibility and cooperate in decision making.
3) Where there is a real sharing of resources and an interest in the needs of others.

The Social Principle has at least three key elements: cooperative work, accepting that human relationships have a karmic basis, and freely chosen dedication to personal development.Each of these relate directly in their effect to the three dimensions of social life, which we are focussing on here. The Three Essentials and the three pillars of the Camphill Movement (König, *The Camphill Movement*) are like tips of the iceberg with regard to ways of describing and practising the spiritual, social and economic realities of life. This can be described diagramatically:

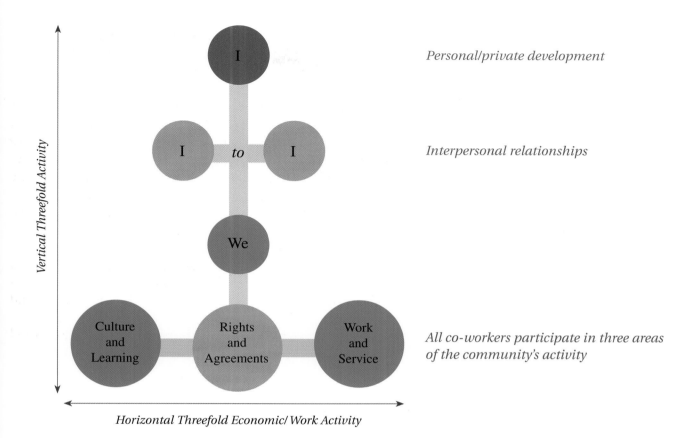

Personal/private development

Interpersonal relationships

All co-workers participate in three areas of the community's activity

Thus, it can be understood that in building community together there is a primary need to work on gaining common moral integrity. This requires continuing efforts at personal development, openness and connectedness between people, as well as a sense of common ownership. If effort is not put into these areas there is a danger of losing touch with the essence, the essence being, as Karl König put it:

> We ourselves must become bearers of this theefold
> social order impulse. We will only be able to do this
> when we carry within us: the free spiritual life —
> *learning*; the economic shere — *working*; and the
> shere of rights — not in our heads as abstract ideals,
> but here in our hearts as an impulse of will.
> (König, *Seeds for Social Renewal*)

I take it from this that understanding has to find ways to manifest in practical affairs and in the ordering of social life amongst people, and this requires us to participate in freely chosen common endeavours. When this begins to happen the distinguishing power of thinking starts to apply itself to the three dimensions we are addressing here, which everyone acknowledges to be their common social context. In this, everyone understands that the aim is the creation of 'a healthy social life' and not only for themselves.

Karl König ends one of his meditations on the Camphill Movement in the following way:

> Once upon a time, the French Revolution intended
> to establish the three great ideals of our modern age:
> freedom, equality and brotherhood. The evil pow-
> ers of French nationalism destroyed these ideals
> and turned them into their opposite. Rudolf Steiner
> revived them again when he proclaimed the idea of
> the Threefold Commonwealth. He described how
> freedom must rule in the sphere of spiritual life, how
> equality must rule in the sphere of rights, and that
> brotherhood is the only possible relation among peo-
> ple in the sphere of the economic order.
>
> Thus in the Movement we become brothers in the
> economic field. We are all equal around the table of the
> Bible Evening, and we acquire our freedom of thought
> in the sphere of the College Meeting.
>
> We share our work in brotherhood, we are equal
> before the face of Christ, we are free as individuals
> when we acquire Anthroposophia. In this way we try to
> become true human beings in the service of humanity.
> (König, *Seeds for Social Renewal*)

Looking at the world today, at the beginning of the second decade of the third millenium, the discoveries in the field of social life made within the Camphill Movement are a significant contribution to furthering the ongoing attempt to realise the threefold social order in practical terms. Despite all that modern life and social theory has had to offer since Steiner's initial insights in 1919, there is a long way to go before humanity will be able manifest 'a healthy social life' in the way he envisaged and the world needs.

Metamorphosis and being

PENELOPE ROBERTS, 1990

George came home from work a little early. It had been a very hot day and he'd been mowing lawns since two in the afternoon. George was good at mowing lawns. He didn't have to concentrate so hard on every movement of his big, stiff hands ... like getting dressed in the morning. It was more work to get his fingers to button every button of his shirt correctly than to mow a whole lawn. Still, he wasn't as easy-going about it as he had been a few years ago, before the accident with the stone. Then he'd been in hospital for days with patches over both his eyes. Lots of people had come to visit, to read or play music to him. But they had been afraid about his eye and that made him afraid too. He'd been lucky, though, and the eye was all right. And he knew how much everyone cared. Since then his eye sometimes bothered him a bit and he worried about it. It was hard not being able to talk about it, and his attempts only produced grunts and bellows. Of course everyone tried to understand and help, but it must be different if you can speak. Well, that was a long time ago. Now he wore goggles when he mowed lawns.

George lurched into the house and started up the stairs to get cleaned up for dinner. He noticed that there was something at the top. Suddenly there was a crash and a scream. George stumbled up the steps, managing to catch the baby just as she was bumping down. Terrified, he picked her up around the tummy with his huge, powerful hands. He was so strong. He didn't know if he could hold her without hurting her, making her cry more. He concentrated on keeping his hands from squeezing too hard. The baby couldn't talk either. They both smiled.

George is a friend of mine. For years I carried this picture of him holding my daughter like a treasure in his great hands. It helped me through many other times when in his terrible speechless frustration he would become a raging bull, lashing out even at those he loved the most. And many times I asked myself, 'Who is George, this friend of mine?'

How many times in the history of man have we asked: What is a human being? How do we define humanity? What is it that makes us recognize the humanity of another? Countless philosophers and scientists have made the attempt to understand, while generation after generation of ordinary men and women, struggling to find meaning in life, have asked the same questions.

For some reason that subtle entity we call 'humanity' seems to shine the brightest when it struggles the most. Perhaps that is why Karl König was so deeply overcome when he saw the handicapped child in Switzerland making its uncertain way so intently around the spiral Advent Garden.

Camphill was born out of the agony of the Third Reich in Germany, the Nazi regime, an era of evil if ever there was one. Yet this evil, oddly enough, sprang from an ideal, the ideal of the superman, the perfect human being.

Just in these years, however, there were human beings who had a different understanding of the pure blood and the whole body. They saw clearly that Hitler in his fanatic idealism had taken the highest picture of humanity and applied it in a completely materialistic way to the concept of heredity. He assumed that the human ideal belonged to one pure race and was passed down through the generations. These others, students of Rudolf Steiner, also held to an ideal image of humanity. For them, however, this was not a visible, racial concept. Through the insight of anthroposophy they had learned to understand that the human *archetype*, the perfect image of man, is a *spiritual* entity to which every human being is related, regardless of race or any other aspect of his or her bodily constitution.

This human archetype is connected with the cosmic archetype expressed in the heavens, the twelvefoldness of the zodiac and the sevenfoldness of the planets. It is related to the kingdoms of nature, stone, plant and animal. It is also an expression of the gestures and even the sacrifices of high spiritual beings who have been active since the dawn of creation. Above all, it is the image of God. God created man in his own image, which is also the image of creation, the Word. The pure body and the pure blood are those of Christ in every human being. Here on earth the perfection is never achieved. Only to a degree, some more this way, some more that, does any living person outwardly manifest the perfection of the spiritual archetype.

Karl König was one of those who seemed to experience the spiritual image of man behind every human being, especially those whose outward appearance or behaviour was the most disturbed. He always saw what was being hindered from coming to full expression. For this reason he was a great healer, but he saw further; he did not stop at being a doctor; he saw another step to be taken.

In the thirties in Germany, Hitler's ideals engendered fear and hatred and eventually the dehumanization of social life. What would be the possibilities for social life if men and women were to try to build a society based on the spiritual image of man as described by Rudolf Steiner? Karl König and his friends embarked on a social experiment which is still in process.

For 39 years I have been a co-worker in Camphill. I can try to tell why I came and why I stayed so long. It has to do with the image of man and the social experiment.

For a few years I managed to bathe in the warmth and comfort that poured so generously from my village friends at Copake. But as things happen, there came the moment for accounting. One day I had to face the fact that actually I could also do something in return. With real shame I realized that I had been free-loading, imbibing love as though it were my due and doing very little to deserve it. Thus began my slow, precarious path of inner change. I was on the way to becoming. I realized that the possibility to experience, through the community around me, the need to change, was an essential factor of Camphill.

I believe that a fundamental principle of Camphill has to do with the polarity between what I shall call 'metamorphosis' on the one hand and 'essential being' on the other — a tension between the ever-evolving state of the human being and his society on earth and the eternal, or archetypal realities which exist in the spirit. Hence the paradox that the villagers, those with so-called disabilities, seemed to see my true being and yet it was they who in the end compelled me to try to improve certain characteristics of my temporal being, my everyday self. This is a positive dynamic in community life. The challenge is to discover those aspects of community life which enhance the eternal image and how the individual or the community recognizes its development, its need to change.

The single human being cannot be truly human and therefore cannot be whole and healthy if he or she does not relate to other human beings. Only through others do we experience ourselves objectively. Through them we can realize our greatest potential, but they can also bring out our worst failings. If we have the encouragement and the will to overcome the latter for the sake of the former, then we begin to clear away some of the obstacles in front of us. We become more fully ourselves. Karl König believed that if many human beings could fight for and stand for the best in one another, social life would change. Anything could be done.

What matters is not simply living together, but the way, the form, of living together. The human being has certain attributes in common with all other human beings. He has a body, a soul and a spirit. He also thinks, he feels and he acts or does. Depending on the *social* context he may develop one of these attributes more than the others. For instance, a community of migrant workers has very little opportunity to develop an intellectual, cultural life as all their strength goes to the picking of crops from dawn to dusk and the little money they earn is saved to be taken home. On the other hand, a community of political prisoners may be forced to create a strong social interaction in order to counteract the boredom of empty, workless hours. There are many accounts of the 'universities' that were set up in the prison camps of the Second World War. A community with strong religious leanings provides the individual with opportunities to develop his devotional nature. A harsh environment like the slums of New York creates the gangs which are loyal to one another but basically at war with everything else. Of course these are all exaggerated examples and even within them every individual will develop differently. All the same it seems obvious that the more fully social life can provide the opportunities for individuals to express themselves in different ways, calling forth different parts of their being (head, heart, limbs for example), the more balanced and rounded those individuals will be. This is most striking with those who are not so mobile in society, such as our disabled or disturbed friends. The most moving experiences I have had in my years in Camphill have had to do with the surprises that come when a person who is difficult in one realm of life suddenly shines in another.

Through the possibilities of encounter in the many forms and settings, discoveries are made. 'Is that also you? I had no idea!' Every new aspect of the community has the potential to light up the individual in his greater completeness and consequently to strengthen bonds from one to the other. Because the forms of the community are derived from the human form (again: head, heart and limbs) they call upon the whole human being. And because the whole human is addressed, he can become more and more himself.

As everybody knows, living together is not easy. Ask any married couple. It only becomes possible through the conviction that problems are positive challenges which can further relationships and deepen them. Community life is healing when we decide to do this, when we do not run away from the people who make things hard for us, but take the opportunity to work the problem through. This means getting involved. In so doing a number of things can happen. More often than not we come face to face with our own prejudice and weakness. We also usually discover quite unsuspected secrets about the person, the one who was so difficult. We begin to see how he sees the world, what his hopes and dreams may be or his fears and doubts. This can happen with anyone, an ill child, a disturbed young person, one of our colleagues, any other human being with whom we have chosen to share our life and destiny. Because we chose in freedom, just as in a marriage, to live with this person, we are able to call upon something greater than ourselves to work into the relationship. We can call upon the higher being of the other as well as our own and allow both our lives to change.

The image of man is not static. Image is perhaps a misleading word because in fact the archetype of all life-bearing forms must include their existence in time. This we call biography. We have an outer biography and also an inner biography. As we progress from childhood through youth to the many further stages of life, we go from one world view to another and to another. At times our very personality may seem to change. So much can happen to one human between birth and death.

In choosing to live in a community with others, we chose to share life. This means sharing biography, being willing to accompany others through thick and thin. It means holding firmly to the faith that each person is more than the particular temporal manifestation we see before us. It means being convinced that although he may be living out his particular way of being as a child or a teenager or person who struggles with mid-life uncertainty, he is all the time trying to become the free individual that he really is. Surprising things can happen. The apparently hopeless teenager may become an outstanding adult; a backward child may develop later into a genius. Without extraordinary insight we can be easily deceived by the outer phenomena. We can form such a fixed picture of the other person that we help trap him in a stage of his biography. Only faithfulness to the true individuality within a changing picture helps him to avoid being trapped, and can allow him to *become*.

In a similar way metamorphosis is also a phenomenon of community biography. Members of a community need to have the same kind of faithfulness to the individuality of the being of their community and its ideals as they should have to one another over the years. This is all the harder because communities include the complexities of many human beings all at different stages of development and with differing perceptions of the community itself. A community is born when a group of people begin to live and work together. They are few. There is little need to have formal meetings because they are always together. Soon they become an efficient organism, harmonious and radiant with the united intentions of those first pioneers. This young community attracts others. It doubles in size. The harmony, the intimacy is harder to achieve. Some feel left out. There are disagreements, opposite opinions. Now there is the need for more objective meeting grounds to reach consensus over community matters. In time these meeting spaces become part of the life-form of the place. They become habits. In the meantime more and more new people come. Some of the originals leave. The origin of the community forms and the ideals which once filled them is but a dim memory to most. Some begin to question and criticize. The community must undergo a kind of life crisis in order to find new forms appropriate to its age. And so on. Without the courage to change, to risk metamorphosis, sometimes at the very deepest levels, the community would cut itself off from its living spirit impulse. It would become an institution, automatic and dried up. The very effort of those living together to fight through again and again to the perception of the guiding impulse that brought them together can become the lifeline to the image of man, the image of community.

The image of man stands always above each one of us, but each of us also has to suffer the trials of earthly life, our own illness, our own darkness or deformity, be it of body or soul or spirit. We need others to love not only what we want to become, but also to love who we are now, so that the illness can be healed, the darkness dispelled, the deformity understood. Such love is engendered by confidence in the positive working of destiny. Such love, if it lives in a community devoted to the needs of human beings, will ensure that its forms will always be flexible and evolve according to the many-sided humanity of those within it.

I said that I would try to describe why I came to Camphill and why I have stayed all these years. For me it was always connected with my growing understanding of the spiritual image of man and the community response to the needs of the individual. Such a response must grow out of human hearts infused by love which flows as a force of life from human being to human being.

Bible Evening

JAN MARTIN BANG

In all communities regular meetings can strengthen the bonds between members, and in the Camphill communities most households celebrate a Bible Evening once a week. The members of the house meet in a 'sublime realm' as brothers and sisters, in the true light of the spirit. The usual form begins with a ten or fifteen minute silence, the members of the household then eat a simple meal together after which someone reads a short section from the New Testament and this is discussed.

Bible Evenings can be grand or simple. They are not religious ceremonies or worship. They are certainly no substitute for church going or any other religious ritual. A Bible Evening is a household celebrating togetherness. According to Karl König, it is a preparation for the Sunday service. But it can equally be a preparation for understanding one another across divides of religion or ideologies. It can be a preparation for living together in this multi-cultural world. Most of all, it is an aid to living together in a household with a number of quite different people.

In 1940 the male founders of Camphill, then living in Kirkton House, were interned as potential 'enemy aliens' for a few months. The internees had nothing very much to do in the camp on the Isle of Man. They found this to be a good opportunity to immerse themselves in a Bible study programme. One night König had a dream where he found himself taking part in a meal with Count Ludwig von Zinzendorf, the founder of the Moravian Church. A conversation developed with König as the pupil and Zinzendorf taking the role of teacher. Zinzendorf suggested that every Saturday evening people should gather to eat and read the Bible in fellowship and try to understand the text in the light of anthroposophy.

König was born into a Jewish family in Vienna, but had been profoundly attracted to Christianity from an early age. In his late twenties he had broken with the Jewish tradition and moved mostly in anthroposophical, medical and intellectual circles. In the late 1920s he fell in love with and married Mathilde Elisabeth Maasberg (Tilla), who had grown up in the Moravian community of Gnadenfrei. Through his reading, and through conversations with the Maasberg family and other residents at Gnadenfrei, König was made aware of the connections between the Moravians and their founder Zinzendorf.

Tilla grew up in a family that gave her a deep and serious understanding of Moravian life, and there can be no doubt that König learnt a great deal from her. It seems that the very idea of working with handicapped children was something that Tilla had started, and that maybe König picked up from her. The seed of the idea of Camphill was first laid in König's consciousness by this encounter. According to König, there is no doubt that the Bible Evening is a direct continuation of what was alive in the Moravian Church. The Bible Evening is a legacy from Zinzendorf.

When König told the community of his dream encounter with Zinzendorf, it was greeted with scepticism and doubt. Despite long discussions, often continuing late into the night, it took a whole year for it to be accepted at all. The first Bible Evening was held at Camphill House on August 30, 1941, with just ten people participating. It was held irregularly at first but gradually, over the years, it became a weekly practice. New members of Camphill Community were accepted at Bible Evenings; it was one of the central poles around which Camphill Community revolved.

By 1949 there were over fifty regular participants. It had become too big, and a fundamental change was introduced when it was decided to split up the group and hold Bible Evenings in every household of the expanding Camphill network. This was forced upon them by the founding of a new Camphill school in the south of England. The co-workers wished to take the Bible Evening with them, and the need to split into two led to the decision to hold it in each household. Up till this time it had been a centralized affair with König asking people to contribute to the discussion. Those who felt moved to say anything at Bible Evenings had to ask him beforehand. As each household held its own celebration the rules became a little more relaxed.

The Bible Evening was beginning to take the form that we know today, and this was further reinforced when it was opened up to whoever wanted to participate. After Botton Village was established in 1956, the Bible Evening changed again, being celebrated by households of adults rather than in the Camphill school setting.

If a community is indeed a living organism, it must contain some 'hidden seed' that is its soul, its spiritual entity, its identity. This is something that needs nurturing, feeding and cultivating in order to stay alive and healthy. There are a number of ways of doing this. The Bible Evening is one of them. It provides household members with a space, outside the ordinary run of their everyday lives, where they can practise equality, bearing in mind that many Camphill residents are people who need help in organizing and managing even the simplest things in their lives. The Bible Evening creates a common language, a place where people can talk and listen to each other.

From its beginnings as a dream experienced by König, through the difficult first years when it was hardly accepted by the other co-workers and was in any case practised by a closed circle of dedicated people, today the Bible Evening has spread throughout the world. Many people have taken part. It continues to be somewhere participants can learn, through deeper listening to others, what they have to say and share. It has become a place to celebrate ongoing community building. It has become a defining feature of Camphill, and a place where equality can be practised amongst members.

In the future the Bible Evening could expand to include a larger understanding of the world we share with so many other kinds of people and their beliefs. It could become a space where we enter into an open dialogue with those people who find their way to Camphill who are not necessarily Christian. To listen to one another, to discuss differences, to try to see the world, even for just a moment, through someone else's eyes and thoughts, is a valuable lesson in tolerance and understanding.

Today there is a burning need for community, a thirst for getting together with other people and creating groups which understand, support and inspire each other. People need to learn to listen and live in peace. The Bible Evening is a social tool which can help with this. At the same time it creates culture, a Camphill way of doing things, from group to group, from generation to generation. If Camphill can continue and develop the Bible Evening, it will help to maintain Camphill's own culture and sense of community.

Building blocks

KARIN VON SCHILLING, 1990

Part of the heritage of European culture that one occasionally comes across is a mighty cathedral. There it stands, in greater than human dimensions and formed in thousand-fold details in spires, pillars and statues. Who built such a cathedral? Who was the master builder? Who were the innumerable workmen and artists? Their selfless service was done for little remuneration, given for the glory of God and the use of people to come, and the fact that no names were added to their works adds spiritual value to the cathedral.

Camphill has been in existence for only a brief time compared with these great cathedrals. But one may still be led to make a comparison. The Camphill Movement is not a spatial, geographically confined, physical building, and yet it has its specific structure, its earthly places and its significance in a specific century, the twentieth century. In this age — which struggles with the seeming polarities of individualization and community, of uniqueness and equality, with isolation and communes — a master builder and his co-workers attempted to create a structure in which people can live. Dr Karl König was the master. He created the master plan in terms of what one may call social architecture and his collaborators helped to bring it about in earthly reality. Today everybody can know of it. Its content is the Camphill Movement. To bring it about required the will for the good. It required 'bricks and mortar' in human terms.

When some of us young people arrived in Camphill, Scotland, after the Second World War, we 'became' the bricks. The mortar that kept us together was the needs of the very many severely handicapped children given into our care.

It is relatively easy to be enthusiastic about fine, futuristic images. But it was not comfortable being a brick! A brick has little opportunity to make advances on the road to self-realization. It is placed were it is needed. Indeed that was the first demand: that specific likes or even gifts had to be sacrificed. Many of us shared our bedroom with a group of children — 'our' children. One of the seven or eight beds in a dormitory was for one of us! I need not explain what a tall order that was for acquiring tidy habits and self-discipline. Order is the firm base for everything spiritual. We worked where it was needed. We cleaned on hands and knees. It was customary that each one had to take over one of the big kitchens for at least one term, whether we had experience in cooking or not. It was an excellent but hard school in many respects and it taught us that one's security is not to be found in outer things, but only within. Endless examples could be given of how rigorously any possessiveness was curbed. We changed houses as the need arose, and that was often, for the first fifteen years. Many of us, I dare say, had to forego dear wishes to move on to further enriching training places elsewhere. But we stayed on. We knew we were working to create a new culture in answer to a great need of our century. Rudolf Steiner put it into these words:

> The sacrifice of his own separate being,
> of his own life, the man must bring
> who will behold the spirit's purposes
> behind the senses' revelations;
> who dares to let the spirit's will
> stream down into his own.
> ('The Soul's Probation' Scene Seven, *The Four
> Mystery Plays*, translated by Adam Bittleston)

We had great examples, first and foremost in Dr König himself. His early successes promised a brilliant career as a doctor and researcher, yet he sacrificed this to forming a community, a movement, that grew slowly because it depended on the free will and individual growth of its members — its bricks. There were also his collaborators, his friends: Thomas Weihs, a gifted young doctor who spent seven years working on a small farm with delinquent boys; and a painter, Carlo Pietzner, who worked for years with children with severe spasticity, to name just two. Their real gifts matured greatly by giving this freely-willed sacrifice. All this was contained in the small word, 'work.'

However, we were certainly not to drown in practical work! There were the other two basic needs: devotion and spiritual striving. The unique contribution that the master builder Dr König gave us was the introduction of social forms. Without them nothing would have been achieved, even if each 'brick' had been aglow with warmth and goodwill we would have remained a pile of bricks! One of Camphill's greatest contributions is to allow individuals to grow mutually in social encounter. This requires *form*. Three social forms were introduced and practised. They grew out of the needs of our everyday lives and appear directed to the work in our schools and villages with handicapped people. However, if one has lived with them one recognizes their value far beyond their present use in our places. They are: the discipline of the college meeting; the Bible evening; and the implementation of the Fundamental Social Law as formulated by Rudolf Steiner.

The Fundamental Social Law crystallized for us the aim of not claiming the proceeds of our labour for ourselves. Outwardly this was applied in terms of a no-wage agreement, thus it pertained to the economic sphere of human life. But our whole life was coloured by it, including the interpersonal human sphere and cultural life. This led to the continuous effort to be willing to pass on to others what one might have gathered as achievements or expertise. The first group of pioneers gave us a shining example of this and it culminated outwardly in their willingness to pass on the leadership responsibilities to groups of younger people. These 'older' people were in their late thirties and we were in our twenties! This sacrifice was hard for them too, but it made the growth of the worldwide Camphill Movement possible.

The three basic conditions — work, devotion and spiritual striving — permeated the three social forms: the college meeting, the Bible evening and the endeavour to implement Rudolf Steiner's Fundamental Social Law. Through such striving each person could forge armour that resisted the temptation to spiritual arrogance and prevented us from losing sight of the essentially Christian message of anthroposophy.

It is impressive to look at the manifestations of the Camphill Movement, but I believe the key to its further growth will live with each individual who is prepared to allow his life to be governed by the three 'building' disciplines as described above, for inherent in them are the words of Rudolf Steiner quoted above. The intent to do this can only be born in individuals who wish to counter the overwhelming social problems of our time with the recognition that Goethe put into words: 'One alone can do little, but if one joins others at the right time much can be done.'

My hope is that coming generations of co-workers will not feel frustrated or shackled by the weight of what has been achieved in the first fifty years. I hope that they will accept this heritage and realize that their searching gaze must look higher into other areas of need where work, devotion and spiritual striving may be applied. May they continue to join hands with the many who have striven to overcome powers ... not in flesh and blood, but in high places (in the words of St Paul), 'so that the healing will of Christ may prevail.'

Spiritual and religious life in Camphill

ANGELIKA MONTEUX

> Camphill is inspired by Christian ideals as articulated by Rudolf Steiner and is based on the acceptance of the spiritual uniqueness of each human being, regardless of disability or religious or racial background.
> (Camphill Mission Statement, UK)

Throughout the history of Camphill this statement has been accepted as expressing an essential aspect of Camphill, indicating that Christian ideals, practices and attitudes lie at the heart of our cultural, religious and spiritual life.

This is interesting considering the fact that many of the original founders came from a Jewish background or considered themselves atheists. Some had actually not held a bible in their hand, as Thomas Weihs, one of the founders, often mentioned in talks and conversations. (unpublished notes from a Michaelmas lecture, 1980)

We know from Karl König's biography that these individuals who had already formed the youth group in Vienna around Karl König in the late twenties studied and performed the Oberufer Christmas plays at a time of turmoil, danger and political and religious persecution during the Second World War. The simple piety of the images helped them to find strength and comfort in these difficult times and strengthened their attempts at community building 'in the light of the event of Christ.' (Selg, *Karl König: My Task*) This could be seen as one of the seeds of Christian ideals in Camphill.

Another seed came from the traditions of the Herrenhuter/Moravian community which were embedded into the practical, spiritual and cultural life of Camphill by Tilla König who came from this background.

Yet another seed was planted through the study of Rudolph Steiner's work and his understanding of the importance of the Christ impulse for humanity. This informed the striving, hopes and ideals of the founder group who wanted to find ways to counterbalance the chaotic and destructive forces at work in the world when they began their new life in Scotland. Activities such as the Bible Evening, services, seasonal celebrations, individual and group study, as well as regular practice of inner development and spiritual striving were established and became a characteristic and essential aspect of Camphill life and traditions. These activities provided a source of inspiration, strength and shared identity throughout the early years of establishing Camphill and later on in expanding the movement worldwide.

It is important to understand that this strong Christian framework is based on an understanding of Christianity that looks beyond the historic person of Jesus to the universal spirit of Christ, who is not restricted to religious traditions, forms of worship or certain established churches. He is rather understood as a cosmic spiritual force, available to all human beings who want to connect to his impulse of bringing unconditional love and respect for the spiritual reality of each individual, and the will to do good here in our everyday lives, actions and human encounters.

In practical reality this means that every action can be given a spiritual, universal Christian quality, guided and penetrated by the love for the other person, the environment and the well-being of humanity. This gives a special meaning to everything that is done on the land, in workshops, in the home or classroom as well as to each human encounter. This can be seen as the true 'religion' — to re-connect to our origin in the spiritual world through our engagement with the physical world and each other.

It also means to be willing to face difficulties, crises and obstacles instead of trying to avoid or escape them, and to see these challenges and trials as opportunities for new growth and transformation — to take strength from Christ's example of accepting death and transforming it into new life.

These Christian ideals and attitudes inspired the formation of the religious/spiritual forms and traditions essential to Camphill communities, and were carried and supported by the active commitment of those living in the communities.

In recent years, however, a process of change has begun. As everywhere in the world, so also in Camphill a change of consciousness and attitude is taking place. There is more questioning, possibly less certainty about the meaning and value of traditions, and also a search for new understandings, new forms and a longing to connect to other spiritual endeavours and other religions.

This lives in many communities in Europe, evident in the fact there are places where few or no Bible Evenings are held, and where services and traditional celebrations are carried by a decreasing number of individuals.

This could be seen as a sad decline and loss of original values. On the other hand it is also a sign that Camphill is not isolated from events in the rest of the world and that the time has come to accept the challenge to explore new ways and a new language of expressing the ideals of Camphill in a changing environment.

Now, in the 21st century, an increasing number of people have a strong aversion to what they perceive as old and restrictive forms of regulated religion, and hesitate to engage the traditional religious life of Camphill, such as the services and Bible Evenings. They are, however, more and more interested in and searching for a spirituality that is open to diversity, respects differences of understanding and manifestation, but at the same time recognizes the universal spiritual reality in all cultures and religions.

This emergence of new perceptions and questions is by no means present in all communities. At this point it seems to be especially strong in some older communities in Europe, those with the longest history and strongest traditions. Maybe this indicates that a certain level of maturity can give a community the confidence to expand its horizons. It seems to be equally true that the newer communities, which are still in the pioneering phase, find strength, support and inspiration in adhering to the original structures and practices.

This shows the great and growing diversity of the worldwide Camphill Movement and poses a challenge to any attempt at pronouncing clear definitions of what a Camphill community is.

This challenge becomes even more acute since Camphill initiatives have begun in eastern countries in a very different religious, cultural and spiritual environment, as for example in India and Vietnam (see *Camphill's outreach into other cultures*, p. 215).

Difficult but interesting questions arise regarding the inner essence of Camphill and the role of Christianity within it, for example, 'Can a place where the spiritual and religious life is informed by Buddhism or Hinduism be recognized as a Camphill community?'

Some are convinced that the original Christian framework and forms of worship should be maintained as the foundation for the work of Camphill; others concede that as long as the life, work and spiritual practice in such communities manifest the wish to safeguard and foster the divine/spiritual essence of each human being, they should be embraced and taken into the fold of the Camphill Movement.

Thomas Weihs formulated this already in 1975:

> We must endeavour to equip all those who stay here
> and who leave us with the powerful and intense
> enthusiasm for the good, for the dignity, the divinity
> of human existence on earth. Thus we may live up to
> the task that is laid upon us.
> (Bock, *The Founders of Camphill*)

This does not mean that differences would be ignored and that the essence of Christianity and other religions would be lost, but that a new effort is made to understand the individual contribution of each religion and culture, and learn to respect and appreciate different manifestations of Camphill's religious and spiritual life.

It will most likely take some time of reflection and dialogue to begin to find the way forward. This will, however, be essential for the future; the example of initiatives in the Far East shows that there is a wish to expand the Camphill Movement beyond its western geographical and cultural boundaries and to respond to the call of those in need of help and support in other parts of the world.

There is hope and enthusiasm in the growing search for a spirituality which transcends outer forms, traditions and rituals. Going back in history to some original sources of Camphill's religious traditions can support this search.

Count Zinzendorf of the Moravian Brotherhood, who was nmed as one of the three stars of Camphill by Karl König is quoted as having said:

> Nature is full of different creatures of different
> inclinations, and it is the same in the spiritual world.
> We must learn to regard various ways of thinking
> as something beautiful. There are as many religious
> ideas as there are believing souls, so we cannot force
> everyone to measure up to the same yard stick. Only

God, according to his infinite wisdom, knows how to
deal with every soul.
(Bang, *The Hidden Seed*)

He related this to different churches within Christianity of
his time, but could this now be transferred to the relationship
between different religions?

This is what Rudolph Steiner said:

Spiritual Science, when considering individual
religions, does not look at outer rites and ceremonies,
but at the way in which the age old universal core
of wisdom is contained/manifest in it. The religions
are so and so many channels which allow that which
was once poured out evenly over the whole humanity
to shine out in single rays ... and if we really search
this essence/kernel of truth in all religions than this
leads to peace. No religion, when truly recognized
in the light of spiritual science, wants to impose its
own special ray of truth on another religion ... All
nations and religions on earth can belong to Buddha,
the great teacher of the highest truth. And all nations
and religions on earth can belong to Christ, the
divine power of the highest truth. And this mutual
understanding means peace on earth. And this peace,
this is the soul of the new world.'
(Dietler Ed., *Anthroposophy and Buddhism*, author's
translation)

And last, but not least, Karl König in 1942:

The encounter with what is spiritual is not a 'Sunday'
matter nor is it confined to festivals; it is a matter
of daily presence of mind. It is not only a question
of own effort; we must not trample on the efforts
of others. It may be that the effort of the other is
greater and more to the point than one's own. One
must have the grace to accept it or else one might, in
disregarding the effort of the other, prevent the flow
of the spiritual.'
('Early Images', *The Camphill Community — A Chronicle*)

With this, he was addressing individuals within one community. Can this now, in the 21st century, be a call to individual communities within the worldwide Camphill Movement?

Will it be possible to find ways to create a global network of Camphill communities, held together and inspired by a universal spirituality which transforms that which is potentially divisive and sectarian about religions?

Tom Ravetz, when referring to the Christian Community — a sister movement of Camphill — says:

> A new unity is born — not a simple oneness, but community, the place of common life, of common work and striving. This is ekklesia, the assembly of those called out to perform a service for the world. They overcome the great divisions that splinter humanity — in Christ there is neither Jew nor Greek, man nor woman, slave nor free, says St Paul (Galatians 3:28) ... This human community is neither uniform nor exclusive. It is not regimented, 'churchy' in any old sense. It celebrates all creativity that is in tune with the abundance of life and love which is the ultimate reality. It seeks for the truth about the journey that we are on, not to prescribe a dogma but to help human beings on their journey. At the heart of the community is celebration and rejoicing.
> (Ravetz, *Free from Dogma*)

Maybe all those committed to the values and ideals which inspired the beginning of Camphill, and who now wish to find new ways for the future, are together on this journey from the original unity, via diversity, to a new unity.

Using the Karl König Archive for the future

RICHARD STEEL

Dr Karl König, the founder of the Camphill Movement, was a very forward-looking person. He researched into an incredible array of subjects and was always aware of and appreciative of research that went on elsewhere. His subjects ranged from specialized medical themes like the function of the inner-secretary glands to history, biography and art. His first fields of study at the University of Vienna were however zoology, botany and embryology, then a very new science. These themes ran through his life like a golden thread. Whatever he turned to there was the underlying question of healing — healing of the individual, healing of the earth and healing of social life. Many new ideas flowed into the development of Camphill but this was for him just a beginning, an 'experiment' as he once put it. All that he did and studied he saw in the light of a far future and urged that one should not stand still but move on, developing those beginnings further and making them fruitful for the future of humanity.

Until now only a small part of König's work has been published and the spectrum of his literary estate has hardly been assessed, let alone utilized for publications. A small group of very dedicated friends and co-workers has done extremely faithful and inestimable work in sorting, classifying and evaluating the tremendous volume of documents, including manuscripts in various stages of over 1500 lectures König held all around the world, diaries and notebooks dating back to König's youth, poetry, preparation notes for planned publications, hundreds of letters and essays, sketches and pictures.

At the turn of the millennium it became clear that a new phase needed to begin and this could thankfully be introduced through the support of Aberdeen University. The complete contents of the Karl König archive could be put onto microfilm for inclusion in the National Archive of the UK; thus also setting the stage for digitalization and a new level of accessibility.

For the 66th birthday of Camphill, in 2006, a start could be made with this new phase and an edition of König's Collected Works were planned, starting with both the English and German languages.

The move to Camphill House near Aberdeen took place in 1940

König's study

Left: Trustees of Karl König's literary legacy from 2006: Christoph Hänni, Dr Stefan Geider, David Coe, Richard Steel, Friedwart Bock

The newly ordered twelve sections of the Karl König archive and publications are:

Medicine and study of the human being
Curative education and social therapy
Psychology and education
Agriculture and science
Social questions
The Camphill Movement
Christianity and the festivals
General anthroposophy
Spiritual development
History and biographies
Artistic and literary works
Karl König's biography

Karl König's original rooms in Camphill House, Aberdeen, were altered to suit modern usage whilst simultaneously conserving as much as possible of the original fittings and special atmosphere.

In cooperation with the Ita Wegman Institute a 'study and research archive' was set up in Dornach, Switzerland, close to the Goetheanum and also in historic settings where the British artist Edith Maryon had lived. This contains copies of the original archive documents in a user-friendly system. In addition an internet presentation of the archive with constant updating of news and information was set up and a regular newsletter started.

The crucial question can now be taken up: how can König's ideas and ideals be made more available and fruitful for the society of today and tomorrow? The archive does not wish to become a storage place for bygone days, but a space for lively encounter, encouragement and inspiration for our social future.

The Eurythmy House designed by Rudolf Steiner was the home of Edith Maryon and now contains the Karl König study and research archive

Camphill today

MICHAEL LUXFORD

I began writing this in the last days of 2009. The last four months of 2009 had seen me in Camphill communities in California, USA; in Ontario, Canada, and at a meeting in Norway attended by communities from Latvia, Estonia, Russia, Finland, Sweden and Norway. In the first part of 2010 visits to the Republic of Ireland, France and possibly Russia are planned, as well as visits to communities nearer to home in the United Kingdom.

That such possibilities are available says something about the resilience of the movement and its recent development, particularly in Eastern Europe, including Poland and the Czech Republic. Since 1990 the work in Brazil has come to an end at the same time as links in India and Vietnam and elsewhere have been developing.

It is not my purpose to make pronouncements about how the Camphill Movement has been faring in the last twenty years, but I would like to take the opportunity to share some thoughts within the context of the dramatic changes which have taken place in the wider social and global situation in which the movement continues to exist, work and develop.

It can be understood that the development of any organization, community or social enterprise mirrors the biographic stages of an individual's life. If this is the case, then at this stage the Camphill Movement would most likely be showing signs of winding down its activity, even becoming infirm, in addition to being able to share its achieved wisdom with others. Inevitably, the decline in physical and life forces leads the way to eventual earthly demise.

Looking at the movement in this way there are developments which indicate a loss of earlier qualities and activities. It would be unreal not to acknowledge this, as change is inevitable and necessary. For example, in parts of the movement the self-management of communities solely by life-sharing co-workers has given way to carrying this task with employed administrators and managers in ways which would have been an anathema thirty years ago. There are pension schemes, senior co-worker apartments, less in-house produced cultural life, even less anthroposophy, in some cases. On the other hand, communities are much more of the world.

In London in 1923 Rudolf Steiner spoke about a spiritual law which says that cultural impulses must be allowed freedom in which to develop out of their own sphere of initiative, but that eventually what develops must find a way of becoming part of general cultural development, otherwise its impulse will have a detrimental effect on the world.

It is my view that this developmental picture of integration into the world is one of the guiding images which describes the existential biographical motif of Camphill today. Camphill will not survive through resistance to the world and by being what many have seen as relatively closed communities. The effect of this law is that what is developed in freedom and relative enclosure begins to integrate its 'discoveries' into partnerships with others.

The last twenty years has seen the growth of general anxiety and insecurity in the world, exacerbated by the post-millennium attack on the Twin Towers in New York in 2001. Tragic events continue to take place in the Middle East, Asia and elsewhere, and issues to do with climate change and sustainability of the well-being of planet earth have become mixed in with financial and economic instability. These factors have left humanity facing important moral and practical questions, which are epitomized by the vast differences appearing between the quality of life of the world's rich and poor.

Such discrepancies remain apparent in the way the needs of children, young people and adults with disabilities are met or not, as the case may be. In most of the so-called developed north, recognition of the needs of people with learning disabilities, mental health and other special needs is well developed. Significant levels of support, financially and in social and medical care terms, is available, at least in principle. Elsewhere in the world this is less likely to be the case, and in the developing world there is much progress still to be made.

As an international not-for-profit organization mainly active in the field of learning disability, Camphill has not expanded to any great extent in the past twenty years. In some situations increasing levels of regulation and quality assurance requirements, as well as the aging of founding co-workers and a reduction in young co-workers staying on, have limited the possibilities for expansion.

Therefore, questions are asked whether Camphill is still relevant. After seventy years of 'good work' is it perhaps entering its elder years and may it, like some other idealistic, cultural and social enterprises, see its founding impulse begin to fade out? With the aging of its third generation of co-workers and the new social policy positions regarding people with disabilities, is it possible that Camphill is no longer a forerunner in the provision of education and social care? There is not space here to expand what could be said to these important questions, though they are the kind of questions which I would expect to be asked as part of the self-reflection by a mature Camphill Movement.

At this point I would like to point the reader to what Karl König, Camphill's founder, had in mind before it began, when he wrote a letter in 1938 to the Irish Government describing his hopes. (This letter is of its time and used the terminology of the day, which would now be unacceptable. Despite this, I have extracted some of his key concepts.) Writing of the person with special needs, he says:

> They would find a community in which they would be able to live and to take up the tasks and the work which is within their abilities.
>
> The aim should be that these children and adults would be united under the guidance of those who put themselves at their disposal into a self-sufficient place which can become a community answering the needs of these people, and which could be self-supporting to a larger or lesser degree.
>
> The necessary foundation of such a community is a purposefully led farm. In this way the work on the land is the foundation of this settlement.
>
> The institution will pay normal prices to the farm from its income for the produce the farm supplies, and in the same way it will also pay normal prices to the tailors-shop, the laundry and the cobblery for their work. The workers in agriculture and workshops receive their wages, if possible, not in cash but in kind — like food, clothing, accommodation, care and medical treatment, etc.
>
> It will be necessary to take care that a small amount of pocket money is paid weekly to each person so that the items of everyday use (tobacco, pipe, a tie, etc.) can be obtained which are the concern of the worker.

This pocket money serves to link the inhabitants of
the settlement with the world around in the simplest
way possible.

 As for the co-worker:

Each co-worker has to be spiritually free. He works
unobstructed in his special field and he works
according to his own free decision.

And:

The maintenance of co-workers and their families is
an obligation for the institution.
   The co-workers have to develop an inner striving to
strengthen their togetherness and to make them equal
to their task every hour and every day. They conduct
classes for each other of an educational, instruc-
tional and work-directed nature. This will serve their
progress.

About home and cultural life he says:

The daily life of the whole house shall be ordered
very exactly. It begins and ends with a short
celebration. Meals are taken, if possible, in common;
the work in agriculture and workshops must not be
disrupted thereby. Communal day rooms, a library, a
hall for dramatic work (a theatre) and other facilities
should gradually come about.
   Thus the meaning of work can only be the
following one: to serve the striving human being so
that he may become ever more strongly a Christian,
in sacrifice and devotion, and as a healer receive
blessing.
   An institute of this kind would be unique and
would stand in good stead in the country where it is
established.

In the seventy years since Karl König wrote these thoughts,
Camphill has indeed found its way into many countries and in
the years to come maybe more will be added, including areas
with different predominant spiritual religious paths.

In visiting many of these communities, particularly in the past decade, my experience has been that the basic elements of König's pre-founding vision remain present, even if transformed, as is to be expected, as a result of ongoing new insights. These qualities and approaches are to be experienced in the voluntary service given and shared with people having disabilities and special needs, in the relative simplicity of life-sharing and in the internal economy of work and financial resources, in regard for the land and environment, and in the continuing commitment to personal development, individually and by the body of co-workers.

What König emphasized about the significance of work on the land, the sharing of material and financial resources, and how to work associatively with decision making, remain directly relevant to the kinds of questions facing the global village of today.

Thus, I believe that what Camphill has achieved on the basis of its founding impulse in these seventy years can be seen as a beginning and not as an end. In a time when there is so much uncertainty in so many areas of life, examples of experienced community living which provide security, worthwhile work and spiritual value for people with disabilities will be even more necessary.

With this continuation in mind, it is acknowledged that people with disabilities and special needs, and the poor and disadvantaged, as König puts it, are fellow-travellers.

Many thousands of children, young people and adults with special needs, their families and co-workers, young and old, have by now lived in or been connected to the Camphill impulse. Of these, many have left and made their way in the wider world, taking with them a strand of experience forged in the particular atmosphere of Camphill. In this process the founding impulse has matured and transformed, and despite the challenges which communities face internally and in relation to external influences, I am sure the movement will continue to integrate its approach to service into the world in constructive and even unimaginable ways.

4. Life Extracts

Introduction

CORNELIUS PIETZNER

The majority of this chapter is taken directly from *Candle on the Hill*. Some of the voices are no longer with us. Others have moved on and are no longer within the Camphill orbit. Yet others have moved within the communities. We have also included some more recent 'extracts.' However, if you didn't know that twenty years had passed between the telling of these tales, it would be hard to distinguish them. The varied accounts of village life, culled and collected from villagers, co-workers, family and friends from several continents, stand as timeless reflections of life in Camphill communities.

These reflections have something archetypal about them, like vignettes of how life was, or, maybe more importantly, how it could be. Perhaps there is a part in us that longs for something these vignettes represent — a sense of meaning, of belonging and place, of contribution, friendship, vocation, community, contentment. It is precisely the specificity, locality and focus of many of the descriptions that encompasses and implies something global, something for all of us. The uniquely individual testimony speaks to what is human in us. In the detail of each mosaic the whole image is reflected, and the totality is comprised out of the unique colour, shape and placement — one could say, 'contribution' of each single one of the parts. In this sense these images of community and village life reach into our souls like short stories or evocative still-lives, creating a broad tableau of connected human destinies and biographies.

Camphill villages: a way of life

There is a wooded, quiet valley in rural upstate New York. There are some old red barns, cows graze in the outlying meadows, and a brook runs through the valley. A peace-drenched, seemingly forgotten place, it is the home of Camphill Village. When you enter this village in the valley, you enter a certain timelessness.

In the heart of the village, glowing red through the trees, stands a strikingly faceted, thoroughly modern building: Fountain Hall. Below it lies the hall pond, quietly reflecting the ever-changing village life. In spring, this is the place to catch the first signs of new life: squirming tadpoles and salamanders. In the summer there are picnics, games, folk dancing and cacophonous bullfrog choruses. In autumn it gathers wind-blown russet leaves, and in winter it hums with skaters.

Fountain Hall is the gathering place for this village community. Its vaulted interior hosts cultural, artistic, educational and social activities. The village assembles here to celebrate a festival, a wedding, a special birthday. Musical gifts are shared through concerts, choirs and speech choruses which resound within its walls. Sometimes guest performers entertain. Plays, skits and pageants are performed, and it is a place for meetings, lectures and common study. The community gathers here for worship. Like rays from this centre, footpaths reach through the woods, over the brook, past fields, across the road, uphill and down, leading to neighbourhoods of houses, the old barn, the new farm complex, craft shops, co-op store and garden. Within this landscape more than two hundred people live together in a therapeutic community. About half are adults with special needs.

Come, choose a path, walk down it and enter this landscape. How soon someone comes to meet you. Come, take a tour. Your guide greets you with an ear-reaching grin, an energetic and prolonged handshake, and bubbling vivacity. She seems proud that you have come to see her village. The way she talks, you might think she owned the place. And in a way, she does.

Along the way, you pass a tall, determined, rather elegant man intently guiding a profoundly handicapped woman down the country road. Suddenly, he drops her hand, spins around three times, bends down, picks up a leaf and crumples it between his fingers. He sniffs it, gingerly, then goes back to fetch his charge and proceeds with renewed determination. You meet many people on the way to work, and they check your progress repeatedly.

> 'Who are you?'
> 'Nice day!'
> 'You happy?'
> 'It's my birthday tomorrow.'
> 'You like it here?'

There is openness, friendliness and warmth.

Climb the hill to the Birchtree workshops, a high, light, modern complex of three craft shops. First you go to the candle shop; such fragrant peace reigns there. Some workers carefully dip candles, others sit around a table polishing, trimming and packing them. Then you come to the book bindery, an airy and calm shop full of quiet industry and concentration. People are cutting, folding, sewing, gluing. There is a pile of handmade books covered in fabric woven or batiked in the village. The enamel shop is next. The room is painted a bold fuchsia, and hanging plants bloom in the window. Here sits our pirouetting friend, calmly polishing copper. Others are involved in the various stages of enamelling. The work-master gets down from his bench to greet you. There are some finished products on display, bowls and platters with transparent, flowing colours and forms. What unexpected beauty!

'Come along,' your guide suggests, 'there's much more to see!'

You meet a baker along the road who is still aproned and capped in white, carrying a bright blue bucket of fresh loaves. Someone else approaches, does not stop or even raise his head, but only continues on slowly, buried in solitude. An officious looking gentleman passes. He nods rather curtly, checks his timepiece, and moves right along with his attaché case under his arm. An inspector? No, he is the village courier, delivering internal mail and messages.

Do you hear that loud 'Ya-a-hoo-o-!' echoing down in the valley? The farmers are bringing in the cows from pasture. One farmer wears an unusual three-cornered hat — his T-shirt —wrapped around his head. The other has a broad, contagious grin. If you follow their footsteps, you would come to Sunny Valley barn where you could watch them hand-milk their cows.

Haymaking and gathering straw bales at Botton Village

Here come the gardeners; their wheelbarrows overflow with spinach and onions. One stops, picks up a basket of vegetables and carries it into the house. He wipes his muddy boots, hastily, and proceeds through the boot-room inside. Would you like to go inside too?

You wander into the living-dining room. There is a round wooden table set for twelve with a vase of fresh flowers in the centre on a hand-woven cloth. The window-sills are filled with plants and crystals. Original artwork adorns the walls. Your guide pops into the kitchen.

'Hi,' she says. 'How was my soup this morning? Did you like it? What are you making for supper?' And then to you: 'I work here in the mornings and today I made borscht. Here is my work-master.' You meet the housemother with a crew of helpers. They might be preparing supper, making jam, churning cream into butter, or beginning to process the newly-delivered basket of vegetables. Someone may be cleaning out closets, ironing or mending.

'Well,' your guide says, 'I've got to go back to my workplace. They need me now. It was a pleasure to meet you.'

If you had really taken a tour of the village, your guide would have made sure you had also seen the wood shop, the doll shop, the bakery, the weaving shop and the garden. You would have been reminded to stop at the gift shop on your way out of the village. Indeed, you would have been invited into a village house, where you would have been received by a housemother, offered refreshments and the opportunity to ask some of your questions:

> 'What is this place, what is Camphill?'
> 'What are you doing?'
> 'How do you do it?'
> 'For whom?'
> 'Why?'

Wanda Root, Camphill Village, New York, has been a co-worker in England and America for many years. This contribution originally appeared in Village Life, edited by Cornelius Pietzner, Neugebauer Press, 1986.

About workshops

Once in a while a special occasion comes around. When Camphill first started it was very special for Karl König, as he had left the war behind and was able to focus his particular talents on a new peace. Those of us who now live in Camphill may well give pause, and endeavour to think where we might be if Camphill had not been started. In many ways what I write now is but a 'thank you' from all Camphill dwellers for the existence of Camphill.

When I first started to work in the pottery, at the start and end of the day I would meet people who were going to the woodwork shop or weavery and so just in that short meeting of maybe five minutes we found a common identity, a common ground; we had become one of a kind. I personally find it very tricky to separate workshops from the farm and garden, now that I come to think about it. People go to work in the farm and garden just as much as they do in the workshops. Many a time the people in the workshops have been asked to give a hand with the harvesting or fruit picking, and it is nice to meet people we live with when they are in their own element. More often than not I have been working in the pottery and I have had visitors from the farm and garden and heard them comment on the skill required to make or throw a pot.

Do I find it commonplace to have our own vegetables? No, I personally find it pretty special. I suppose what I am trying to say is that it really does not matter what we do as long as we do it. So now comes that distinction between what we do, and what we do well. Many people would probably not believe that they possess special talents. I know when I first met pottery I was happy to do almost anything because I found the pottery, or 'place of work' a nice place to be in. I was fascinated by the wheel and showed enough interest to have a try.

I met workshops as a whole before I met pottery. When I first came to Camphill it was in Glencraig and it was so that a newcomer had a week in a workshop and the next week in another workshop. This was to try and find where a person would be most happy. I found this in itself pretty special because it is not so often you like your work. As a rule work was just somewhere you were put and you did this job or you were 'out.' This was a great pity because it is so that your work can be the ruling factor in a content life. Spend the day from 9 to 5:30 doing something that is not to your liking — many people either quit or it becomes automatic to them; the one is as detrimental as the other.

When people take their time to find out what work you are happy with, then something happens. A challenge comes around. I think many people find this to be the case. A job which was just a job becomes something more. We tried to make a better job out of an ordinary run-of-the-mill job, and that was because the effort was appreciated. This is very much an important point and probably the point at which work becomes important. The challenge to do a job of work well is appreciated, not only by the person who does it, but also by the person who asked for the job to be done.

When I first went to work in the pottery I noticed that care was taken in the work you were given. At first you were given a job that was well within your capabilities. As you progressed and you were having success the jobs were subsequently more difficult. There came a time when the choice of work was left to you. I think this was quite a testing time because it was assumed that you had been taught enough and therefore your proficiency was enough to let you get on with things, without instructions! This state of affairs can be very nice but, oh, it isn't nice when you are simply told to do twenty mugs followed by thirty candle-holders! The point being, I suppose: 'Get good enough, and your responsibility goes up by half.'

I think the main difference between farm and workshop is the small amount of space between you and your fellow workers. Tolerance is the key word! There is no space to walk away from whoever because Monday is treating them wrongly. However, remember your own imperfections and take into account that your neighbour might well have a headache, and you are halfway there. What we must remember is that by going to our day's work we have proven to ourselves that we are capable, and capability is a very important factor to all of us.

John Porten, a resident in Hapstead, Devon.

Glass engraving, Botton Village

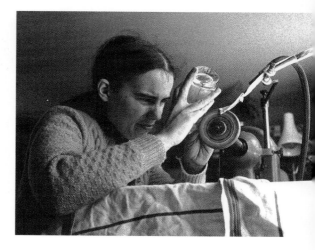

Work and rest at Botton bakery

News from the bakery

I started to work in the bakery just before Christmas. Michael Balcombe used to be the baker, but he decided that he wanted to do something else. He had been the Grange-Oaklands baker for a number of years. Then Norman came to take over the bakery and Michael has been showing Norman the ropes. I must say it was nice watching Michael teaching and showing Norman what was done in the bakery. In the bakery there are several other people besides myself working. Angela, Andrew, Karl and Susanna work in the bakery in the mornings, also not forgetting Norman.

They start at around 7:00 in the morning or even earlier when Norman or Susanna light the ovens and start doing the dough. When it's about 8:30 then the bakery gets into full swing, busy making granary rye, honey salt, white bread, rolls, wholemeal or whatever is needed on that particular day. On Mondays a member of the bakery cleans the hall ready for the service, but then on Tuesday afternoon I can be seen delivering bread around the Grange and also at the end of the day. We put Oaklands' bread on the transport. Each week we pack Thornbury and Cherry Orchards, which are other Camphill places. We make special bread for festivals and also for the service (white). We have had increased orders from houses which means we have been very busy trying to meet people's needs.

Some people from outside have been buying our bread which is very nice indeed. I just thought I would write the prayer which the bakers say at the end of the day. One very nice thing is that visitors have commented on the bread and how nice it is.

Prayer of the Bread
O Raphael be our helper
By thy power of healing
Restore this weakened grain
May the power of the sun
Be in the gold of the crust
May the power of the air
Be in the rising of the leaven
May the warmth of our love
Add strength to the loaf

I'm afraid I don't know who wrote this prayer, perhaps the person wishes to be nameless. Norman and his happy band of bakers wish you happy eating and if there are any questions, please ask. Barbara is making new bread bags as the other ones are getting too old or are too small for the bread.

Thank you, Barbara, for making the bags.

Sue Donat, a resident from Grange Oaklands.

Baking in a Camphill community

Baking bread is a very responsible job for our everyday consumption within the community. The whole process of baking begins with weighing flour, adding salt, water and yeast and then comes the mixing of the ingredients in a bowl. Now comes the kneading process which transforms the whole mixture into dough (gluten). We press with all our strength using the palms of our hands and when the dough becomes lighter and bounces back when we touch it, it means it is ready. Then we put the dough in a bowl to let it rise and then we cut it into loaves. We knead the loaves and put them in tins to rise for a while, then we put them in the oven to bake for 45 minutes, then we take them out and there we have our finished product.

Andrew Graham, a resident in Grange Oaklands.

From my days in Grange pottery

There had been a crew of four to six villagers who had stayed with me in the slow and hard learning process in the craft of pottery. In the course of many years some of them had achieved a good overall skill and a consciousness for the whole complicated, manifold working process. In this way a very good cooperation had developed between us, resulting in a considerable production of great variety.

The time of the year passed in the rhythmical change between feverish work and more relaxed periods when it was possible to deepen and perfect abilities and to practise new ones.

It began straight after the summer months with the strong push towards the Christmas sales which started in October, the conclusion of which was our Advent sale in the Grange. The other activities could stand in the foreground — no more rush till after the Holy Nights. There followed a time of steady production which filled our storeroom to its utmost capacity so that we were wondering where to put the next lot that came out of the kiln. But then the shops began to stock up for the summer business. Newton Dee craft shop was one of our best customers. It was a relief to see everything disappear as it always did.

There was usually a happy, often hilarious, atmosphere in the workshop. And indeed there were some unforgettable characters among us. Michael was the ever beaming sunshine of the place, sometimes with priceless remarks which, however, are difficult to relate to people not knowing him. Sometimes I was startled hearing a lengthy conversation going on next to me between John Canning and Innes Foley, co-workers supposed to be on business elsewhere.But it was only Jeremy who, bent over his work, in a one-man show, imitated the voices of these two gentlemen holding forth about the state and treatment of Grange motor cars or other subjects, in an absolutely perfect way. Or there came suddenly the many noises of a whole flock of sheep, big and small, interrupted by the neighing of a horse, the mooing of a cow and the penetrating shriek of a circular saw, all produced by the voice of A.R.L. with an incredible genuineness. It was the same A.R.L. who gave to our products the characteristic touch with his astonishing variety of beautifully executed engravings on mugs, dishes, jars and bowls. There was also gentle, friendly Ben with his wonderful care. He often came over after supper to take things out of the moulds or to cover them up to prevent them from getting too dry overnight. Never would he let any of his products perish, in contrast to Mary, who never remembered what had to be done with things coming off the wheel. And there was the faithful Sylvia who I knew from her school days at Newton Dee. She thrived in this company of originals, until after ten years she wanted a change and went to Botton.

So life went on in the pottery for twenty years. Some of the dear old friends left, but some remained steadfast. It was they who made it possible for the workshop to carry on even when I was finally called away, and a succession of different people took over the pottery with more or less knowledge of the craft — but the faithful potters were there to tide over. This, I think, is the greatest credit to them and deserves to be mentioned when we look back at the development of Camphill.

Erika Opitz, craft-master, Grange-Oaklands.

A day in the life of Beannachar garden

'Morning! Me again! Keep on going, don't stop!' Dominic is obviously ready for work this morning. I find him a large space where he can dig to his heart's content and return to the garden shed where others, less industrious, are slowly gathering. A small group settles down to string the onions into skeins of golden globes to hang under the rafters for winter. The sun shines and the work goes easily, one to rub off the dirt, one to sort out the good from the bad, one to twist the skeins among the string.

I take a group to clean a weedy patch of ground ready for autumn sown broad beans. 'Alan,' I say to a reluctant teenager, 'could you bring a barrow for the weeds?' Alan turns his back and runs out of the garden. 'Alan! ALAN!!' Sounds of stampeding feet beyond the garden wall. Some minutes later he reappears, grinning apologetically, wheeling a squeaky wheelbarrow.

Two heads of hennaed hair move above the beans and rounding the corner two ex-co-workers drift into view. 'We are here for a few days. Can we do anything?' In the greenhouse juicy red tomatoes are falling off the vines, and beside the path french beans grow longer and tougher. It is good to have a few extra pairs of hands.

The lunch bell goes and everyone downs tools. Some only too literally — a fork flies into the bushes, a hoe is dropped into the weeds. These retrieved, we troop in to remove welly boots and wash hands.

The afternoon begins. The cook, wearied after his morning's labours, wanders out hoping for a quiet moment. Another co-worker, whose love is any machinery but especially the tractor, takes an enthusiastic group whooping with joy off down the drive to collect leaves for compost and branches for sawing. Everything has settled down nicely with no mishaps, except that Kylan has fallen into the flower bed again. A lorry laden with straw roars up the drive followed a few minutes later by an excited group of leaf rakers. Everyone rushes round to the farm and bales of straw are passed from hand to eager hand. Most of it ends up in the barn safely under cover, but a few broken bales remain to litter the yard and are swept up by conscientious hands. The rest of us return to the garden. Half an hour before supper, what shall we do?

Some return quite happily to their jobs and peace reigns again. Others, less settled, help to gather vegetables and deliver them to the store ready for the cooks tomorrow.

'Hard work! Hard work!' puffs one, laden under a full basket of leeks, their green leaves trailing like seaweed around his shoulders and under his arms.

Yes, it is hard work, but when the day's work is done and we troop in for supper we can stretch our feet under the laden table and feel a good day's work has been done.

Celia Baldwin, Beannachar.

A work day

I have a very good working order. In Newton Dee village I think many people do. My name's Raymond Friskney, rather a strange surname, isn't it? There's so few people with such a surname. I come from Grimsby town — a fishing port. It was a major fishing port at one time.

My work, like most villagers except for the farmers and bakers, begins at 9:00. We usually have breakfast at 8:00 in Orion where I live, and have lived for over fifteen and a half years. I just won't leave Orion; I like it very much. In Orion we have seven other people: Pamela Watkins, Peter Mason, Helmella, Emma Jackson and Susan Furth, who's been in Camphill centres since she was a child. We have a child living with us, and Irene.

I work in the store with Vitus and Valerie Werthmann, who are in charge, and Martin Harris, their right-hand man, Guy Sproat, the shadow boss, John Blanchard and Mark Hughs and Viola, a young German co-worker who is with us for a year. We make up orders for the schools and the village and have lots of outside customers.

Work stops at 12:00 and then I return to Orion for lunch and help to set the lunch table.

In the afternoon I work in the laundry with Simon Blaxland de Lange in charge, and a co-worker called Gerlinde who lives in Roadside Cottage. The rest of the team are as follows: Ingrid Hughs who also has a sister called Margarete who lives in Capella with Valerie and Vitus; Eleanor, who lives in Morven; Tony Pitman, who lives with Simon in Lyra; Pamela Watkins, who lives with me in Orion; Audrey Rae, who lives in the farm. Sometimes Flora MacFarlane, who's also in Lyra with Simon and Tony. We have a young man from Murtle called Alexander who does the folding and works on the spin drier filling it up.

Various people deal with different parts of the laundry work. Most people can fold the sheets, tablecloths and duvet covers and pillowcases, but the ironing is usually done by a few people: Ingrid, Eleanor, Pam, Gerlinde, Simon and myself. Pamela does most of the finishing touches and puts the laundry on to the various shelves where it goes.

We pack the laundry on Friday mornings and deliver it to the Camphill school estates in the afternoon.

So that's my work routine for the week and we have talks and other activities. In the evenings I mainly read maps and novels.

Raymond Friskney, a resident at Newton Dee.

Blessings on the meal

'Oh, good and bad, good and bad'

I suppose it all happened on December 26, 1961, that I, as a rather nervous new villager, entered Botton for the first time and the start of a new life, so totally different to — and to have a profound change on — what had been my life up to then.

Some months before, I had gone to Harley Street to be interviewed by Thomas Weihs and it had been agreed that I would go for a trial holiday of two weeks. The only thing was that 'two weeks' has turned into some 28 years that I have been associated with Camphill, a thing I had no idea of at the time, nor do I suspect did the many long-suffering co-workers and teachers that it has been my good fortune to meet both now and then. Perhaps 28 years is rather a long 'trial holiday!'

So there I was at the threshold of a new life, which up till then had been pretty pointless, now to be met by not only a point to my life, but a challenge, as I felt deep within my inner being called upon to a realization of an acknowledgement of my higher being, for whether in the cultural life, work life, or just on the daily contact of being a true human being, I was met by true human understanding.

Not that my early days at Botton were easy, far from it as I had to come to grips with the mirror reflection that was Michael Parker which, as I say, was no easy task, but still the many co-workers I came into contact with held up that mirror and said, 'If you cannot accept the image that is cast there, change it, don't just sit around and bemoan your fate, do something about it.' And so, by degrees, and with the help of the whole of Camphill, I was able to change it, I hope, for the process is still going on some 28 years later.

It may be wondered what has made the most impression on me out of my association with Camphill. Is it the work routine, or perhaps the plays that celebrate the Christian year, or just the community life that is led in school, village training centre, or halfway house (all of which I have had some experience of at one time or another within Camphill)? It is none of these and yet it is all of them, for the one thing that I carry with me always is the one thing that embraces them all, namely that which makes Camphill unique — the Bible evening. For there we are occasionally privileged to see behind the veil, and to have a glimpse of the spirit realm as man stands out as what he is supposed to be, and through him we are able to experience the finger of God as it writes on the hearts and souls of those present, be they villager or co-worker, or like me, just a guest. And one sees over and again the pulsating heart of Camphill beating to the eternal rhythm, and the life of the community starts to make sense, as one participates in the ever-renewing wonder, and you know that you are part of the whole, part of the community.

It can again be wondered why I have called these reflections of life in Camphill 'Oh, good and bad.' That's soon told.

It was the first time that I met Dr König, and that was back in February 1962 after he had given a lecture at Botton on the special constellation that had occurred at that time in connection with the thalidomide child. I was introduced to him as a new villager by Peter Roth, and he said, 'Ah, so you are the Michael Parker I have heard so much about,' to which I replied, 'Only good things, I hope, Herr Doctor.' He just simply said, 'Oh, good and bad, good and bad.'

Well, all I can say is as I look back now on my association with Camphill, there have been far more good than bad memories that I carry with me. I look at the one-time little community that now bestrides the globe like some great colossus, as Camphill has come to embrace many countries, creeds and cultures. This must surely be its true memorial, as friends and well-wishers celebrate its Golden Jubilee, and help it on into the 21st century, and beyond.

Michael Parker, a resident at Botton.

An outing

The climb to the Scottish castle had been strenuous, and we let Alice, our 52-year-old friend with Down's syndrome, rest on a chair we found outside the locked ticket office. As it was midday the office was not manned, and we proceeded to climb the tower of the ruined castle. When we reached the top and looked down, we saw Alice looking with a smile on her face at the shining coins in her hand. We wondered what had happened and then saw another group of tourists who had arrived after us and given their £1 entry fee to our would-be ticket lady. Alice transferred the money to her pocket with a friendly 'thank you.'

Axel Stutz, today the principal of the Karl König School, Nürnberg.

A discovery

A short time ago I made a discovery — I noticed that the children living in my parents' house are handicapped. Looking back into childhood, I see children and adults living in my parents' house. I was a child and belonged to the world of children. We had our do's and don'ts, our likes and dislikes. We climbed trees together, roamed the world together, fought and had fun together.

At nine and a half I went to boarding school. My school friends changed, but we were still children in a children's world. I do not remember them as being different to the children at home. As I grew older I started to baby-sit and then housekeep at home, the typical lot of the eldest child. At some point I must have registered intellectually that I was 'different.' But I have never quite known 'different' from whom or what? I have always been me.

I went on to train and work as a social worker and eventually returned to work in Camphill. This summer I spent some days in my parents' house, my childhood home, and was surprised to see just how handicapped the children are who live there.

I asked my mother, 'Were the children I grew up with in our house as handicapped as these children?' She looked at me and smiled, full of amusement at my perplexity, and said, 'Yes, dear.'

Veronica Hansmann was born and raised in Camphill and has worked in Blair Drummond, Scotland.

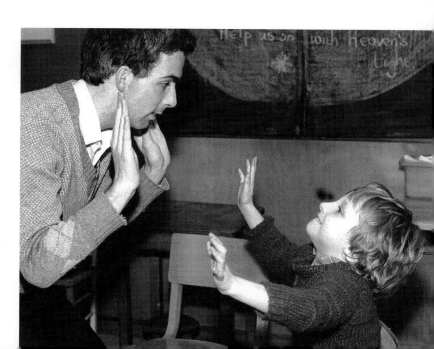

The way of my brother

My brother, Jonathan Gitlin, arrived on October 5, 1956, plunking himself down in New Rochelle, New York, in the midst of our family: my stepfather Harry Gitlin, my mother June, and my older sister Cathy.

Jon's birth was surrounded by a lot of confusion. There were tests, conferences, talking with doctors. We were finally told that Jon was a Down's syndrome baby, somehow different from the rest of us. This confusion didn't end with the diagnosis. A lot of questions remained to be answered: Was he truly? Wasn't he? How severely? How mildly? I was in the fifth grade, and these questions intruded into my life, which was filled with the politics of the school yard and with finding the most appropriate way to drive our teacher out of her mind.

In the first year or so of Jon's life things seemed rather normal to me. I loved having a baby brother, and he seemed happy to be there. I would take him with me in a stroller when I went on errands, carry him piggyback for shorter distances, or around shops and stores, go to the zoo, watch him in the yard. There were other baby brothers around the neighbourhood, and Jon wasn't very different from the rest.

But, by the time he was two, it was clear that Jon was different. He had stayed a 'baby' brother far longer than the brothers of my friends; he had stayed in the stroller for many months longer. He needed things done for him much longer. He didn't learn to walk well. He didn't speak so well. People wanted to know 'what was wrong with him.' Things didn't stay so 'ordinary.' To find my place, I had to change. I had to learn a new way.

Jon taught me. We began with patience, which he taught in a simple and pragmatic way. His reaction to adversity was to SIT DOWN. Immediately. Wherever he was. Completely boneless, limp. He would just flop down. And in that position he was a dead weight, far too heavy for me or anyone else to lift. This smiling baby brother, who five minutes before I had been carrying on my back, was now as ponderously heavy as the Rock of Gibraltar, and as impossible to move. My strength could not lift him. Cleverness was wasted on his resistance. It took patience, love, comfort and understanding (and a sense of humour), in strong doses, to transform him back to a manageable weight.

Jon taught me to see others in a clearer light. He was my barometer. Jon evoked a reaction from everyone. Nobody was immune. And these reactions revealed each person's character. He was slow to develop, and behind his age group physically, verbally and in independence. Even at five and six he had to be pushed in his stroller, and couldn't express himself in a manner which was recognized as 'normal ' No one escaped reacting to him, even if only for a fleeting moment. And in that reaction each person's psyche was revealed, and nothing done afterward could change the truth of that vision.

I began to decide certain things based on those reactions: I wouldn't shop at certain stores, because the owners' reactions to Jon were not kind or understanding. I judged the adults around me in the manner in which they related to Jon. Some patronized him, although at the time I would have said they just acted stupidly, and couldn't communicate with him directly.

But there were those who just accepted him and loved him simply. Jon's grandmother was one. A Russian Jewish immigrant, she had no notion of Down's syndrome: what it meant, the genetic truths which underlie it or Jon's future. She just loved him and took care of him, just as she did the rest of her grandchildren. She has a permanent place in my heart, not just for this, but for this as much as anything. Our brother Sam, the youngest of the family, accepted him. As Sam quickly outraced Jon and surpassed him in physical and mental development, he quickly shifted gears and became the protector and older brother.

Still, Jon was an outcast. The society in which he found himself had no place for him. His behaviour was disquieting, his abilities too limited for him to find a comfortable place in state school or in special education classes. Our mother did yeoman's work. New Rochelle, where we lived, had not lived up to the laws of New York State, which mandated the specifics of special education for children like Jonathan. So began the battle of the Board of Education. My mother, always a fighter, devoted herself to eliciting, by whatever means necessary, a proper compliance from the local authorities. Day after day, week after week, she fought with them; by letters to Albany and Washington, by letters to her legislators, and finally, by the most powerful means possible, learnt from Jon himself. She sat. In the waiting room of the superintendent of the Board of Education. Immovable. Knitting and sewing, reading and just waiting. Day after day, from the moment they opened until the moment they closed. Until finally they agreed to see her and fulfil their obligations.

Even so, Jon had not found his right place. He had helped to make sure that many children like him would be properly cared for in the state education system, but it wasn't his place.

And then a small article appeared in a local paper. Word was passed from parent to parent. A lecture was going to be given on disabled children — no, it was always 'retarded children' — and on Camphill Special School, this 'place' in Pennsylvania where everything was different. It could have been a notice for the appearance of Peter Pan, or an invitation to Never Never Land; it grabbed the attention of a number of parents who had been searching. They went to listen, and sat spellbound. It was Carlo Pietzner who then appeared. From that moment there was no question in my mother's mind as to where Jon should go. Interviews were set up. Carlo sat in a motel room and interviewed, not the parents, but the children. He had long and meaningful conversations with Jon, and with a number of other special children. A decision was made. They would go to Camphill.

Jon left home and went off to Camphill Special School in Pennsylvania. There he began a life quite different from what would have been possible for him at home, even with the best of special education classes in the state school system. Living in a house among a number of houses around the village, with other villagers, with houseparents, children and farm animals, he entered a world that slowly began to work with him to evoke that special Camphill magic: to help him find all that he could express, manifest, develop.

My visits to Camphill School left a deep impression on me. There was a quality of life there that was different, brought to me through this younger, 'retarded,' 'disabled' brother. After all, Jon had, from an early age, been teaching me something vital about observing the world around me, and myself, and what might be possible for us humans in it.

Jon was living in Camphill School, first with Erika, then with Adola. Our family visited on Saturdays. I was in California, going to college.

Jon lived in a house at school with his best friend, Alan, whose father and Harry would take turns driving the two kids home and back again for holidays and vacations. Jon and Alan couldn't have been more unlike one another. Jon was compulsively disorderly, and Alan compulsively orderly. My mother tells a story: on a visit one Saturday to the school when Jon was about eight or nine, she said to Adola, 'It must be hard for you having both boys in the house.' Adola replied, 'Well, we strive to have a balance.' Almost as if to demonstrate, the two boys began to play together. In the schoolroom all the toys were kept in cupboards built around the periphery of the room, at floor level. Jon went in a circle around the edge of the room taking out every toy in the cupboard in front of him and depositing it on the floor in the middle of the room. Alan came along right behind him, putting each toy away exactly where it had been. This circumambulation continued without end, until it was time to stop. Balance. Harmony.

A vision of Camphill lodged deep within me: standing on a hill in Beaver Run watching a new house being built. When Jon went to Beaver Run there were only three houses built. More were built 'right under him.' And this: watching kites being flown in the breezes of a Pennsylvania spring. These physically 'unable' children running in the wind, holding the strings and flying their kites high in the sky. And watching Jon grow to be a young man, ready to take his place in a society that was ready for him, in a Camphill village. And watching many 'retarded,' 'disabled' and 'non-functional' children work, study, grow and function. This image, this balanced relationship to others, and to the possibilities inside each of us, rooted itself deeply within me.

Jon grew up. He went from Beaver Run to Camphill Village, Copake, New York, with a couple of detours in between. I moved back from California to New York. My parents had aged. I had aged, also. I married. Had a family and home of my own. The convictions of my youth had faded somewhat. I had made my peace with the urban jungle, and had almost forgotten the vision of Camphill Special School as an island of sanity in a maddening world. Every now and then, though, the image of Camphill would return to me. There were visits to Jon and from him. I would contemplate the future, the purpose of that future. Sometimes I would regret the loss of the hopeful fantasies that had held me during my youth. But Jon, my parents, the entirety of that relationship didn't let that die altogether. Harry was deeply involved in the life of the village and devoted to Camphill. For him it had answered, albeit indirectly, a crying need that I am not sure he was ever aware of. The question of maintaining Jon, and the Camphill villages, as time went on became more and more important to both the villages and the villagers, as well as to the families. Copake needed to start something, or something needed to be started, in any event, to prepare for the next period of time. And Carlo Pietzner, who, some twenty-five years before, had reached out to my brother, reached out to me and others. Carlo's far-reaching vision indicated that the villages, the community, needed to reach out and grow new shoots, sink new roots, or it would begin to stagnate. Something needed to be done to expand the community, to bring in those of us who were too 'fortunate' to have had, by necessity, to go to Camphill. Those of us who now needed to recognize our connection with the choice of destiny that our siblings had made. And we had to recognize that their destinies also connected with ours. We needed to learn to be sensitive to this stream in which we were being carried.

One Family Day at Copake, in the fall of 1983, a group of brothers and sisters of the villagers gathered to discuss the need to continue this impulse. Gathered around the library, ranging in age from late teens to late fifties, married or single, with families or without, confused or sure of ourselves, we recognized that there was more destiny at work here than we had known. Brothers and Sisters of Camphill Village USA started to take shape.

Harry grew quite ill. He was clearly able to do less and less to support Jon or the village. His death was approaching, and by now he knew that. His last sickness, the slow approach of his end, was something in which we all, the entire Camphill family, participated. The village and all about it helped to prepare Jon for his father's death, and to connect us all.

Harry was near death. Jon needed me. And equally I needed him in the way I had come to understand I needed him when he was an infant, and he was my teacher about human reactions. I needed him to guide my spirit as it made yet another slow revolution around the ground beneath it in its search for some meaning to life on earth. I needed him to help me to recognize Camphill. Yes, he needed me too. To continue the relationship between him and family outside the village. To continue to be able to do the fun things with him that come from a visit home, a day out, planning for a Family Day. We needed each other.

Harry had struggled to go to Family Day, in October, 1986. It was difficult for him; he was very ill and surgery was scheduled for ten days later. It was the last thing which he did under his own power. The year before we had organized a discussion on death and dying as the principal activity of Family Day, and Harry had listened carefully as the questions concerning preparing for death had unfolded. He was changed by that day, I am sure of it. At that moment, I think, he realized that he had only a short time with which to prepare, a short while in which to develop whatever would be needed for the next step in his journey.

The village supported him. Through Jon, and through many others. People wrote to him; Kate Meinike sent him a card made of fallen leaves which hung over his bed for the last two months of his life. When he died, Jon and David Tarshus, Sylvia Bausman and Andy König were there, at the house, within three hours. Jon sat by his father and explored his wonderment at where he had gone.

Jon was not just Jon, he was a link to Camphill. And Camphill was not just where Jon lived, it was a link to a search that was my search also. Maybe all who are 'Camphill' don't live in a village. Why did I feel, whenever I approached Copake, or Beaver Run, or Kimberton, that I was going home?

The Brothers and Sisters organization grew. It is quite strong now, each year doing more and more to contribute to the life of the village. There are studies of the anthroposophic basis of Camphill village life on Brothers and Sisters Day. There is the annual dinner dance. There is the growing community which will give birth to brother and sister organizations in other villages, which will someday help to encourage other young people to visit Camphill and possibly to make their lives, or a part of them, there.

There is the deepening bond which continues to grow between the village and us. It is like a tube through which flows communication, love, meaning, intention, destiny, hope. It is something which gives meaning to life on both sides of the connection, and allows activities in both places to be seen in the light of the realities of the other.

Camphill grows more central, day by day, to my image of the life of modern man and what is needed for it to continue. I am a proud server on the Board of Directors of Camphill Village USA, and on the board of trustees of the Camphill Association of North America. There is emerging, soon I hope, a truly American Camphill which will attract a new generation of American young people. And, as I watch Camphill places grow around the world, I wonder how many other times will the birth of some soul like Jonathan lead to such a family journey? There must be Camphill places to allow these stories to unfold. It is an obligation we all share: to continue to allow these special people to weave the webs of destiny with us, around us. Ask Jon. He knows.

Bill Prensky is a businessman in New York City.

Wedding celebrations at Botton

What Camphill means to us

I speak several languages, studied at a prestigious US university, and had a management position in one of the world's top marketing companies. My wife was working too. We were on the fast track and a handicapped child did not fit into our world. But Karl John came into our lives, and he was handicapped. A convulsion and lack of oxygen right after birth caused brain damage and learning disabilities. Hyperactivity and other behaviourial disturbances were the consequence. As he grew up, his disabilities became more and more obvious. Coming home after a day's work or from a tiring business trip, he sometimes got on my nerves. When we went to a restaurant or on a weekend outing there was invariably some kind of upsetting scene so that it would have been better if we had stayed at home.

By chance we got to know John Byrde from the Camphill village Perceval, in St Prex, Switzerland, with whom we shared our worries. 'If you move to Germany,' he said, 'see Hans Müller-Wiedemann.' We did, and Karl John was accepted at the Camphill village Brachenreuthe on Lake Constance.

We were terribly upset about giving our son away. Yet we could hardly handle him any more (which must have been also due to my own immaturity). I was worried whether or not Karl John would be happy at Brachenreuthe. I was worried about him disrupting the peace in his house and in the village. I was worried about the co-workers well-being and whether they would keep Karl John. After all, I knew our hyperactive son!

Having Karl John sit still in a chair for five minutes was utterly amazing to us. And all this without tranquillizers as Dr Müller-Wiedemann predicted? Ha! We expected a phone call any day, saying, 'Look, we tried everything, your son is just too difficult.' And when we asked how difficult he was compared to the other handicapped children (that interested us at the time), the co-workers simply said that they loved him very much.

Well, Karl John could stay. He made enormous progress and became much more balanced. Since then, twelve years have elapsed and he is now living happily in the Camphill village for adults, Hermannsberg, also on Lake Constance. We are delighted. What happened? How was all the progress possible? We wanted to know more. Previously, a famous doctor told us that tranquillizers were the right thing for our son and there would be no harm or side effects.

My wife and I love our handicapped son and we are always happy when he comes home on vacation. But for more than ten years now the pattern has been more or less the same: after a few weeks we are worn out and, I am afraid to admit, glad Karl John can go back to Camphill where we know there is a lot of trust, love and experience. We know that he is more balanced and more quiet at Camphill than at home. At Camphill, the co-workers usually live with up to ten handicapped in one house, 35–48 weeks a year! Where do they get their strength? And on top of it, when we visit them they welcome us, offer cake and coffee and radiate inner peace and warmth. Driving back home from a Camphill village on Lake Constance through the winding roads, the apple orchards and the forests of southern Germany, we always feel a unique sense of joy. Exactly the same feeling strikes us when we visit other Camphill places.

Gatherings, festivals, lectures and conferences with Camphillers and other parents with handicapped children, of which some have become close friends of ours, opened new doors for us. Anthroposophy was not new to us, but because of our many moves, we never gained depth. We wanted to know more and are now involved with Camphill and anthroposophy. It has given us answers, changed our lives and values and given us deeper roots so that we could better master the problems of today's life — of which we have had our share!

Now, the ticks of my son and the other handicapped people no longer disturb me. Somehow they tend to have a positive effect. When I participate in a Bible Evening, look into the villagers' eyes and listen to their simple and pure comments, it dawns on me what Camphill is all about. Thank you, Karl John for opening our eyes.

Alfred S Heinrich is a businessman in Meggen, Switzerland.

The rings of fellowship

The occasion was the third Parents' Conference, the venue, the Grange Hall. Ninety parents were happily exchanging experiences and problems.

'He is so much better and loves his work.'
'But they don't let him have his television, which he enjoys so much.'
'He loved his Granny very much, we could not possibly have taken him to the funeral, he would have been so upset.'
'What a blessing, with scanning and abortion there will be so much less handicap around.'
'But they don't believe in abortion.'

Discussions like this, which raised questions which could only be touched on in a conference, led to the forming of the first Ring in Droitwich in March 1983. A group of about 24, four from within Camphill, met three times a year. They strongly believed that there was a deep-felt need for those 'within Camphill' and for those who lived on the 'fringe' to develop greater understanding of each others points of view.

It was realized that there were many parents and friends who only partially understood the anthroposophical approach to life, and those who were already following the principles of anthroposophy were glad to be able to discuss important issues with those who might hold different points of view.

The subjects discussed have been wide-ranging. For instance, medical ethics and the unborn child; the temperaments; life after death; the threefold social order; relationships, and others.

It has been a great experience to spend three days in a year discussing matters of consuming interest with people who have come together with the bond of knowing a handicapped person, or being interested in anthroposophy. I am sure those who are part of the other Rings feel equally stimulated and rewarded in their discussions.

Jean Davidson

'Mornin' everybody'

Well, ain't the birds chirpin' and the frogs burpin' this mornin'? Somebody around here must have been livin' right, else we couldn't 'a got that nice little bit of rain yesterday. We sure could use some more, but you got to be thankful for what you get.

Say, speakin' of what you get, Steve told me about a note that some or'nary housemother dropped into his box, the one who couldn't do her dishwash, with all sorts of remarks on it listed in categories with numbers. Steve said she must be tryin' to show him she knows how to count.

Well, she seemed to be sort of mixed, happy-sad, because she said that when she finally got her water back, the hot came on faster, and she didn't have to waste a truckload of water just waitin' for it, and why, after all these months of askin' Steve to do something about it, did the situation suddenly get better, when Steve could have raised the pressure long ago and fixed everything.

Steve was stumped. He asked me how you go about explainin', or even tryin' to bother to inform someone like that, about how the pipes in the basement of her house are a tad bigger and a smidge longer than most, and how they get full of hot water when someone is using it, and then all that water sits there when they're not usin' it and cools off. And the real reason it comes on faster is not because of the pressure, but because Tom Sholl (bless his heart and our pocketbook) spent a good part of last week riggin' up a system Steve designed to keep hot water in those big pipes, whether someone was usin' them or not?

She even had the gall to poke at Steve's childhood and say how awful it must have been. Steve told me he had a wonderful childhood. He says he even had a dumptruck just like me, he used to play with in the neighbour's sand box, only it was red instead of green, and that warmed my heart. Then he went on to say I was the only woman he ever wanted to marry 'cause I always did what he told me to do, and didn't never give him no back talk. Then I almost turned as red as that dumptruck Steve had when he was a kid.

Well, I shouldn't be botherin' you with all this, 'cause the real reason I wanted to get into your mornin' mail was because Steve was sittin' there watchin' that rain yesterday when the detective inside of him started scratchin'. Next thing you know, off he goes to see if all those dag-blasted hoses wuz turned off. Now over in the field vegetable patch folks got their act together and everything was fine. But back by Mornin' Star garden, in spite of the fact that there's two houses just a sittin' there starin' out, the hose cocks wuz still on after we'd had a good half-hour of rain. Now that means Old Red was puttin' in extra time. His time in electricity is close to 3,000 watts per hour, which comes to about 33 cents, and that's not a crime, but if you take into account that his days are numbered and the $2000 plus it's going to cost to replace him, it gets a little more stiff. And pumps is famous for going under on a holiday or a weekend when everything costs more, if you can get it at all.

So if you garden folk would work out some kind of deal with the Sycamore Linden folks for if and when it does rain, things'll be better.

'Sophie', USA. Sophie is the name of Steve Chamberlin's dumptruck. A series of articles appeared in the weekly news-sheet of the Kimberton Hills village under this name.

Excerpt from a diary

I am at Camphill Farm and have come for a two-week trial visit. This afternoon I played frisbee with Geoffrey, Anette and a friend. After a good session of fun we got ready for supper, which is very light.

In Labora House there are five of us, and our house-master is Lawrence Adler. The five of us are all boys: Jeff, Gary, Richard, myself and Hamish. After supper Gary and I did the dishes. Then at 7:45 there was an assembly for the forty villagers and staff. Gary is the chairman of the Village Assembly, so he did the address. It was very interesting. There were points on gardening, punctuality, films etc. They also welcomed me to the farm, which I thought was quite something.

Eventually the meeting ended on a good musical note — we sang. Back at Labora House, Gary, Jeff and I had coffee then went and chatted upstairs for a while before turning in for the night.

Monday, April 27: My first day on the farm. At breakfast this morning we all said Happy Birthday to Hamish. Now it is time for action. I start with the farmers. I meet Tim and the others.

There is Charles, Mark, Alan and Grant. Charles and I went to herd the cattle into the pastures. Then I helped Grant clean the cow's kraal ... back to work at 2:30.

Jeff is plucking chickens with Tim and Allen. I went with Charles to fetch the cow herd back to the camp, then we went to get the chickens from the shed to get ready for slaughter. Then we went to the dairy and I took an interest in the milking. The day's work was over at 5:00. Hamish wanted a dance at Labora (for his birthday). A lot of villagers turned up. It was a good dance.

Tuesday, April 28: We went to the goats' paddock and picked up all the dead trees and branches so Tim could burn them in a trench. After work Gary, Jeff and I played table tennis. We were joined for a while by Lawrence. It was good fun.

Wednesday, April 29: Charles, Grant and I helped Tim sow the seeds from the tractor by hand. Then I helped Anne clean the floor of the dairy. Having finished it was time for lunch at 12:00. It was a good lunch cooked by Barbara. Tonight is shop night.

Thursday, April 30: We went to the barn where we milled the grain. Back at Labora we had supper with a visitor, Gary's girlfriend Barbara.

Sports day

Friday, May 1: This will be my fifth day here in the new month of May. Charles and I went and chucked rocks aside while Tim was mowing the grass. Then Mark and I joined Anne in the dairy helping her with the cheese and milking the cows. After supper there was a social evening for everyone. It was a pleasant evening, with dancing.

Monday, May 4: The vet came to test the cows for pregnancy. There were today at least three cows pregnant of five that he checked. The evening meal was fine with tea done by Gary. After supper we played bingo. It was fun — no gambling though!

Tuesday, May 5: I went to the dairy and helped Anne make butter. I did the churning while she prepared the bowls, and so on. While we were making the butter we sang some songs. I was invited to the Old Farm House for lunch, it was very pleasant. In the afternoon there were groups. I was in two: from 2:24–3:45 I was doing folk dancing, then 4:00–5:00 I did music. It was fun, especially the music.

Wednesday, May 6: I went to the dairy to help Anne make yoghurt. Anne steamed the milk in a pot in which I checked the heat with a thermometer. After that we poured the liquid into jars and let it set.

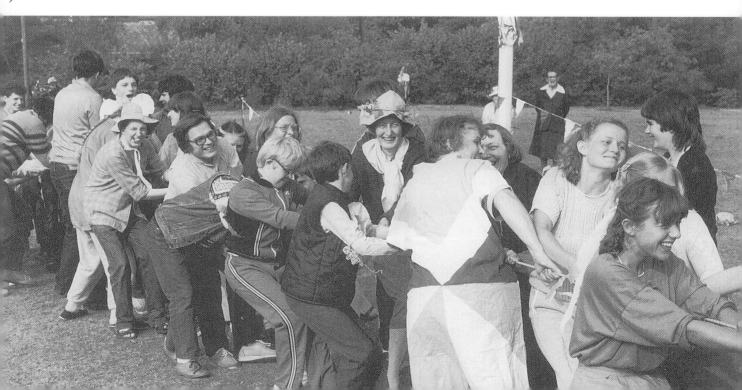

Thursday, May 7: Today it is field day around the houses. Everyone works outside around the gardens. We started digging a trench and filling it with rubble. While Jeff was breaking the rubble I was digging and shifting the sand.

Friday, May 8: My final working day on the farm. This afternoon at 3:00 a bus is coming to collect us to go to Cape Town. We are going to watch some play at a Waldorf school. They will be Greek plays, but in English.

The trip was nice — going through places like Houhoek, Strand and Somerset West. We arrived in time. The first play was about Helen of Troy. It was good. After that there was an interval. Then the final play was a comedy. It was hilarious. After that we started back to Hermanus. We arrived back at 12:40 am. What an evening it was!

Saturday, May 9: The morning's work is picking up rubble for the trench. So off we went in the truck and loaded up with rubble. Then we came back and started working on the trench. Two young kids from Castor, Stephen and Raymond, came and helped us. Eventually I had to stop, as I was invited to lunch at Melissa's house. Ulrike and Tim are the houseparents there. It was Tim I worked for and the reason for the invitation was to say thank you for the work. After a good lunch I said goodbye to my farm friends. In the afternoon Stephen and Raymond played with Jeff, Enorietha and myself. We played frisbee and football.

Evening came, so to the Bible study. I read a passage and put the candle out. The meal was fine for all of us.

Sunday, May 10: My last day here at Camphill. The two weeks have been pleasant and very interesting for me. The morning started at the chapel with a service; then we had breakfast. Now I am packing my bags. In Labora everyone is upset that I am leaving. They are threatening to tie me up to keep me from going, but they know that one day I might come back.

Thank you Labora. It has been pleasant being among true and good people. See you sometime. Here I end my report.

Peter Johnson, South Africa.

The happy cows of Clanabogan!

The farmers in Clanabogan were feeling desperate about their cows. They only had a few cows to milk but these didn't have a lot of milk to give and the people in the community needed milk for breakfast and also for baking cakes. It was up to the farmers to solve this problem!

They asked the cows to please try a bit harder and they tried to convince them with delicious hay and oats, and they were even willing to give them turnips, but nothing changed.

One night, when one of the farmers went as usual for a walk on the farm, to check if all the doors were closed, he passed the cow yard and one of the cows spoke to him: "Hey, farmer, if you want to have more milk from us, you really should think about something special you could do for us!"

So the farmers met and thought about something very special they could do for the cows. "What do the cows want? What would make them happy?" they thought.

They came to the conclusion that they should install a fully-automatic cow brush for them.

The cows appreciated this cow brush very much. Even the cows which were not giving milk enjoyed it and they were so pleased with the brush that they soon calved so that the farmers could milk them and all the people in the community had enough milk again.

If you are lucky you can sometimes even see a farmer using the cow brush!

Anonymous, published in Camphill News, *Northern Ireland, Spring/Summer 2006.*

Farm work

My name is Vika and I am 25 years old

I have lived in Svetlana for many years. I like it here. I take the pig buckets from all the houses to the pig shed, lay the table for lunch in my house, wash the dishes. On the farm I cut up beets with a spade. In the afternoon I work in the paper workshop and the wood workshop. I go to my parents in St Petersburg for the festivals, and I miss the village.

It is very beautiful here.

Lots of guests come and I like talking to them.

Published in Svetlana Village News, *Winter 2006/2007.*

Training and craft workshops make musical instruments and metalwork

Market

I am going to the market every Friday. But I take somebody along. Usually William and Yun Sil are coming with me and of course, Christian as well. We are selling potatoes, beetroots, onions, leeks, parsnips and other things from our own garden. Several times I deliver potatoes to the customers. The market is normally next to the carpark in Ballybay. In winter times I am taking a flask with tea in it along because otherwise is is too cold outside. But we are not only selling things, I am also buying things in the market, like pies for the community or flowers for my family. Pauline picks me up before first teabreak and me and Stephen have to lift the tables into the van. Heavy stuff!

John Robb, published in Ballybay Newsletter, *2008.*

Painting lesson

Left: candle-making
Below and bottom right: carding and
spinning wool

Queen of Camphill meets Queen of England!

It wasn't quite like that, but nearly! Early last summer, when the High Sheriff of Buckinghamshire visited Camphill Milton Keynes, he was introduced to Morwenna Bucknall who had been the first English co-worker to join Camphill, in 1944.

The two of them struck up a lively conversation about Camphill, and about Morwenna's father, who was a socialist priest. Morwenna said something about how we organize money in Camphill, to which the High Sheriff replied, "That sounds like communism." Morwenna responded, "Ah, but with the spirit!"

A few days later I bumped into the High Sheriff at a petrol station when he said, "I've had a mad idea! I want Morwenna to be invited to a Royal Garden Party at Buckingham Palace."

I responded positively, though I was not sure if Morwenna would be too keen on this idea, given her socialist roots. However, when the gold embossed invitation arrived, Morwenna straightaway saw it as an opportunity to get some important words into the hands of influential people.

So, later in the summer, I accompanied Morwenna through the gates of Buckingham Palace to the garden party where we saw the Queen from a distance and Prince Philip close up. Morwenna had brought some extracts from a lecture of Rudolf Steiner's on the Fundamental Social Law, but we did not manage to get them into the Prince's hands and thence to Prince Charles, Morwenna being a long-time admirer of Charles's social and environmental initiatives.

Even so, it was a delightful day — sunny, incredibly English, and the hats were amazing. Morwenna wore a white gardening hat from a neighbouring co-worker's collection. The refreshments were enjoyable, even though I wish people wouldn't cut off the edges from cucumber sandwiches. It reminded me of cricket matches at school!

Michael Luxford, published in Camphill Pages Newsletter, *Issue 26, Spring 2008.*

A village portrait — Fred Malamed

I did not believe at first
that you would walk out of a painting,
without first pausing
to change your clothes
and remove the other traces;
but then I began to recognize
that there had always been
a special quality in your walk,
the hidden genius of a Chaplin
confined to canvas and paint
and constant scrutiny, the self-
awareness and distinct melancholy
of a body fashioned by a brush —
with death.

I saw you long ago
returning from a sun-spent day;
your easel under your arm,
your hat slightly shrunken
and with a giddy tilt,
your shadow drunken on the ground,
a victim of sun and paint.

I saw you as you saw yourself
and as I see you now
when the sun returns, and you,
you amble past a row of sunflowers
without even turning your head,
and yet you always turn to me
as soon as I enter
into painting distance,
your greeting, sunlike, open,
brushing away at shadows ...

but now it is my turn
to paint — your yellow slicker,
worn in the manner of Provence
and only a hundred years out of style;
a bunch of parsley, held
like a bouquet — with both hands —
in place of the cluster of brushes;
and the scrunched straw hat,
put on with both hands too;
and yet I have lost your gait,
it seems to have wandered
far from my canvas, your left leg
lifting, as if freeing itself
from some subtle entanglement.

Andrew Hoy, formerly of Kimberton Hills, USA,
has been a Camphill co-worker for many years.

5. The Regions of the Camphill Movement

What are the regions?

COLIN HALDANE AND RICHARD STEEL

Just seventy years ago, on June 1,1940, the name 'Camphill' was attached to the impulse of that young group of Central European refugees around Karl König. But when he was later asked how old the Camphill *Movement* was, he pointed to the fact that with the first contact to initiatives outside of the United Kingdom (in Helgeseter, Norway) in 1953, one already spoke about a 'Camphill Movement.'

> We already then spoke about the Camphill Movement
> ... Certainly parents speak of their children before
> they are born; we only did not realise that this child
> was not born.
> (*Annual Report on the Movement*, Newton Dee,
> January 31, 1961. Unpublished document, Karl König
> Archive)

Then he considers that the real birth of this 'child' had taken place with his journey to South Africa. In 1957 the first real steps towards a worldwide movement, also into Germany, Holland and the United States could take place.

Until 1964 a 'movement council' met twice a year with König as chairman. Here an awareness of the whole of the movement and its concerns were nurtured and many of the fundamental decisions were made. König himself extended his consciousness in a special way into all corners of the expanding work, a capacity which the other founders also aspired to practise.

In a dramatic moment of the last council meeting in 1964 a change took place which had biographic significance for König himself, but which also gave momentum for the evolving natural structure of the movement. In his report from the meeting König stated that henceforth he would no longer lead the movement but help the developments in Middle Europe. The movement council would be dissolved to make space for the individual steps necessary in the six regions then to be formed (the tender beginnings in Scandinavia were still being looked after by the Northern Irish region). König adds to this step a plea to those wishing to shape the future tasks:

> I beg you earnestly to see this dear friends: to see this new step, to see this new chapter, which opens in the book of the history of the Movement. We are now embarking on a very new venture. Responsibility will be shared on a much greater scale than it so far has been. Freedom of decision for the single one will be given. If this is carried in our hearts and the Bible Evening is common for the whole of the Movement, and in the celebration of the Offering Service there lives the whole of the Movement — then this will be achieved from within, what the interest into each other's work will achieve outwardly. And the Movement will be an instrument for the work of the Spirit.
>
> Dear friends, in connection with this you will understand that the part which I personally played so far has come to a close. You will have to come to regard me in a different way. I am now responsible as chairman for the Movement in Middle Europe, but no longer for any other region. Keep this clearly in your mind. This is also the reason for me to go now and spend more time than I so far have spent in Europe. I so to speak will try to strengthen the roots of the Movement there — because no doubt we have grown out of central Europe.
>
> (*Annual Report on the Camphill Movement*, January 29, 1964. Unpublished manuscript, Karl König Archive)

For each region a chairman was named who would be responsible for creating a structure for cooperation within that region and — because those named were all men — two secretaries were named to form a bridge between the three British regions (Anke Weihs) and the three others (Alix Roth). In this way a kind of archetype was started for that which has since become the Camphill Movement Group, consisting of around nine members, carrying the continuity of consciousness, and meeting annually with continually changing representatives of the now seven regions: Scotland, England and Wales, Ireland (north and south), Northern Europe, Central Europe, Southern Africa and North America.

With the movement not having centralized management or administration and having become an ever more complex and diverse collection of communities and individuals spread across the globe, much of its activity and structures, formalized or otherwise, are often conducted within the regions by and through their various organs, meetings and associate activities. In this sense each region finds also its own means of best meeting and supporting each other, and in turn linking to the whole.

It is within these regional structures and organs where the nurturing of new initiatives can and does take place and it is there that support can be forthcoming. Thus it is up to the individual regions to define what the criteria are for becoming a Camphill community. Clearly reference needs to be made to the wellsprings, origins, ethos and philosophy that lie at the foundation of the movement, while at the same time having regard for what is being asked and what can and needs to come about at any given time and place, and of course, above all, stands the will to work together.

In the following section you will find contributions from the various regions of the movement. Of course they are descriptions from certain perspectives at a specific phase of time — snapshots of a living and changing biography, and, in the sense of the above quote, not only adapting to various geographic and historic situations, but also linked in a special way to the evolving biographies of those individuals the communities consist of.

If you were to visit the various communities you would meet familiar outward manifestations and you would experience some of the less tangible but still familiar feelings and impressions. Whether these communities are small or large, with adults or children, rural or urban, in Britain or Botswana, they manage to be both unique and yet retain a common expression and experience.

This is an expression of the nature of the Camphill Movement and its diverse and different manifestations across the world and its ability to achieve a certain cohesion and uniqueness wherever it lives.

Outside Camphill House

The Scottish region

RUSSEL POOLER AND SIMON BECKETT

Camphill took root in Scotland with the move of the founding group from Kirkton House, near Insch, to Camphill House, a small estate on the outskirts of Aberdeen, overlooking the River Dee. This was in June 1940 and until the 1970s the work of Camphill in Scotland was very much concentrated in the Aberdeen area. This period saw the purchase and development of Murtle, Newton Dee and Cairnlee, all within the Dee Valley and in close proximity to each other, with the work initially focussing on children and adolescents. In 1960 **Newton Dee** was purchased by the Camphill Village Trust and began a new phase as an adult community. **Camphill** and **Murtle** estate continue to provide education for children and young adults from the ages of 3–19 while **Cairnlee** offers further education and training to young adults aged 16–25.

Above: Spering lamb at Milltown
Below: Newton Dee house and garden

Above: Harriet and Martin, Newton Dee   *Below: Blackcurrant picking, Newton Dee*

The seventies not only saw the beginning of an expansion of the Camphill impulse in Scotland but a geographical move away from the north-east. In 1972 **Ochil Tower School** in Auchterarder, an existing residential Rudolf Steiner school, was purchased by Camphill and continues to provide education to pupils aged 5–18 years.

The seventies saw a growing need for the development of further education and training for young people over the age of sixteen. This education and training was concentrated in the arts and crafts, home-making skills and in horticulture.

In 1973 **Templehill Community**, near Auchenblae, began its work as a Camphill community, catering for a very wide variety of needs and age groups but later concentrating on adolescents and young adults (it was to close in 2000). A year later, in 1974, **Milltown Community**, a small residential community, was founded in the village of Arbuthnott.

John and Ingrid Fisher's wedding, Newton Dee

Left: Laying a path, Milltown

Right and below: Joinery at Milltown

Below, far right: Milltown, tools for self-reliance

Blair Drummond, a large Victorian baronial-style building near Stirling, was opened in 1976. The community provides a residential setting and a wide variety of arts, crafts and horticultural training for adults aged eighteen upwards.

Blair Drummond house and some residents

In 1978 the community at **Corbenic** opened, set in the tranquil foothills of Highland Perthshire and near Dunkeld. It initially offered training for young adults but has now developed into an adult community offering residential and day activities based around arts, crafts, horticulture, farming and estate work.

Above: Corbenic farm

Below: Corbenic farm

Left: Wool work at Corbenic

In the same year **Beannachar**, on the south side of the River Dee near Aberdeen, opened its doors to young adults. The community offers residential and day activities in arts, crafts, horticulture and farming to young adults aged 18–30.

A growing need for a community catering for adults in need of greater levels of support led to the founding of Loch Arthur in 1984, many of the founding members coming from Newton Dee Community. **Loch Arthur** is located on the edge of the village of Beeswing in Dumfries. The community of seventy souls offers a wide range of activities with a strong emphasis on the growing, producing and selling of food.

Opposite page:
Top: Corbenic bakery
Bottom: Art at Corbenic

Below: Shrove Tuesday 2009 at Corbenic
Right: Blair Drummond House

In the same year a group of co-workers, responding to the need for elder care, founded **Simeon Community** on a part of the Cairnlee Estate. Simeon provides a community setting for older people in need of residential care.

In 1987 **Tigh a Chomainn** was founded with the intention of providing a small residential setting, allowing residents to find sheltered work in the wider community.

In 1993 **Tiphereth Community** began its work, in Colinton on the south side of Edinburgh, offering a small residential setting and a larger day activity scheme.

At the time of writing **Pishwanton Community**, near Gifford, is working with Camphill towards becoming a Camphill community.

A variety of communities provide a wide range of services to all age groups. The physical presence of the communities is only one aspect. At the present time the Camphill communities in Scotland are responding to a wide variety of changing needs and demands in the fields of curative education and social therapy. It is these responses that give the communities their vibrancy and life and is what helps to make their work so relevant to the needs of today.

Involvement and engagement with the local community is a very relevant and rewarding part of a community's work. In the field of social enterprise we see many examples of this:

Milltown have recently opened a very popular garden centre, which has attracted a great number of new visitors.

Loch Arthur's farm shop sells a wide range of foods, many of which have been produced by the community through their farms, bakery and award-winning creamery (the creamery's Criffel won Best Organic Cheese 2009 in the British Cheese Awards).

Tiphereth works in the Pentland Hills maintaining footpaths, planting hedges and clearing rubbish.

The Colinton Compost Scheme uplifts garden waste from over six hundred households.

Newton Dee with its wholefood store, café, gift shop and bakery attracts ever larger numbers of regular visitors to the community.

Opposite page: scenes from Loch Arthur

Other schemes which involve the wider public are reflected in the befriending and advocacy schemes at Blair Drummond and Corbenic.

The inclusion of all members in all aspects of the life of the community has made some significant strides forward, with residents joining management committees, the growth of student and pupil councils, the development of inclusive conferences, most notably New Lanark.

Working in partnership with other organizations and statutory bodies is another new theme:

The Camphill School Aberdeen have worked in conjunction with Aberdeen City Council to create a Nature Nurture Scheme. This offers early intervention for the under fives from deprived districts of Aberdeen and surrounding areas. The children are offered outdoor play and learning opportunities, which helps to promote an understanding of the natural world, collaborative play, positive learning, self-risk assessment and problem solving.

The St Andrew's Project run by the Camphill School Aberdeen has the purpose of offering extra help and support to children and their families through the provision of day or residential childcare both within and without the child's home.

Tiphereth have begun a project in collaboration with both health and social services. The project entitled Outremer works with individuals with very challenging needs, from secure units, with the long-term aim of helping to get them back to a more normal life situation.

Care for the earth has always been a strong and essential part of Camphill's ethos and so the communities continue their work with biodynamic farming and gardening. The Camphill School and Ochil Tower have both been involved in the national eco-schools scheme. There are many experiments with alternative and renewable sources of energy. The houses and work areas are designed as living buildings to enhance the lives of the people

Opposite page: scenes from Loch Arthur

living and working there. The Camphill Architects, with two offices in Scotland, play a very important part in this.

The creation of the Camphill Scotland office in the mid nineties was of crucial importance to the development of the communities. The office has been able to offer guidance and expertise to the communities, particularly in the areas of government legislation. The services of this office have allowed the communities to be able to enter into constructive dialogue with both central and local government and thereby effect and influence change on both a local and national level. The partnership with government has also led to recent high-profile conferences in partnership with the Scottish government.

The medical and therapeutic interventions offered by the Camphill Medical Practice are of enormous benefit to the Camphill communities in Scotland. The communities benefit not only from the medical expertise but also from the many other services on offer: counselling, eurythmy, speech, art, massage.

The ever-growing need for an innovative and effective approach to the challenges of caring for the elderly has brought the work of Simeon to wider attention. Simeon is and has been pioneering the creation of a community in which each elderly person can contribute according to their individual ability, and in which the dignity of everyone is truly upheld in all phases of life. Simeon Community's expertise in this area has meant that they have been able to help and advise other Camphill communities in the field of elder care.

The training of co-workers has always been a very important part of the work of the Camphill communities, with the first seminar beginning in 1949. The development of this training into the Bachelor of Arts in Curative Education (soon to be called the Bachelor of Arts in Social Pedagogy), in collaboration with the University of Aberdeen, has been a hugely important step in the development of Camphill's work. It has now led to state recognition of the training received by co-workers and has been a significant factor in the recruitment and retention of the next generation of co-workers. There are many other significant courses on offer both within and without the communities, and all play their part in the development of the skills and motivation of members of the communities.

Examples of these courses include: The Adult Communities course, Mental Health Seminar, Kate Roth Seminar, Ways to Quality. A course in Autism developed in the Camphill School is now a nationally accredited Scottish Vocational Qualification Unit.

The resurgence of research and development work, notably around the Karl König Archive, is also of significance for the future of Camphill, as Camphill is able to explain the value of its work to the wider world. The Camphill communities in Scotland have become ever more engaged in working with other organizations, both governmental and non-governmental, in a very positive interchange of ideas and methods. The communities have become more porous as they allow for this interchange of ideas. It is the challenge of the future that this interchange takes place in an open and welcoming manner while at the same time maintaining the identity and ethos of the communities. The future beckons to the Camphill communities with many challenges and demands for change and development. The identity and ethos of the Camphill communities are crucial to the future, but so is the need to be open to the demands of the future. The matching of these two, at times seemingly incompatible, will ensure the continued development and health of Camphill communities in Scotland.

Garden workshop, Tiphereth

The English and Welsh region

VIVIAN GRIFFITHS

Lady in the church hall, Botton village

The region of England and Wales has so many different Camphill pioneering projects that it has become a remarkably diverse region, with school, college and adult villages as well as urban communities and places for shopping, craft, training, and a residential provision for a school not even part of Camphill. The list begins sixty years ago with the idea of the first children's village. It was ultimately started in Ringwood, Hampshire when a parent offered The Sheiling, a house on the edge of the New Forest, in 1954. The **Sheiling School**, with its children's household, craft workshops, gardens, landwork and classrooms was a farsighted project in this sandy pine forest. Yet it was not the first venture south from the Camphill estates on the edge of Aberdeen. This accolade goes to the establishment in 1948, following a request to Dr König, of residential support for the **Rudolf Steiner Special Needs School, St Christopher's, Bristol**. With households established in Wraxall, Somerset and Thornbury, Gloucestershire, north-east and south-west of what was then a bomb-ravaged city with shortages of accommodation, community support for a special school was established. **The Sheiling, Thornbury**, first as Thornbury House and then as Thornbury Park, went on to become a school community, a sister school and children's village to **The Sheiling, Ringwood**.

In 1952 a remarkable meeting had taken place, another first, when parents of the Camphill Aberdeen schoolchildren, rapidly growing up and travelling up and down on the 'Rudolf Steamer' special train overnight to London Kings Cross, got talking in the waiting room (the train must have been late!). This led to asking Dr König at a meeting, appropriately at the Magic Circle Club (the magicians' organization) what they should do when their offspring grew up. 'Start a village,' was the answer. 'You do it,' was the challenge. 'And provide an oasis of culture, work and social interactivity. Develop crafts and a household that respects adults' particular needs; it is not a school.' The meeting was the first step to the establishment of the Camphill

Village Trust in 1954 and soon after came the purchase of the **Botton Hall Estate** from the Macmillan family in 1955 — the second Macmillan property, following Camphill House in 1940. The parents (all except the notable magician Peter Hogg and his wife, who retired from business to run a guest house in Botton village) couldn't give up professional careers, so Camphill co-worker families took up the challenge. Learning not to be a school was difficult and the first group drove across the rainy and windswept North Yorkshire Moors in the autumn of 1955 to a remarkable dale with a hunting lodge and two farms. With no electricity, this new life in rural Yorkshire was a Christian social experiment that was the first of its kind, or so it was believed.

These pioneering community ventures continued throughout the sixties. At that time Camphill was seen by some radical policy makers as the cutting edge of social provision for people with special needs, and initiatives which then began included **The Grange**, a horticultural village community on a Gloucestershire hillside. It provided at first a home for staff children and a place for fruit growing, becoming a village in its own right in the early sixties.

Delrow College and Rehabilitation Centre was established in 1963 near Watford in an old school close to the M1 motorway, replacing the Harley Street consulting rooms in London. Now called the **Delrow Community**, it produced a unique gateway to community life whereby people could come and experience life in a community, and this was especially useful to those who experienced mental health problems.

Carrying the theme of a more urban-based environment, Stourbridge Houses, later to be known as **Camphill Houses** was established in the Midlands town of Stourbridge near the North Worcestershire village of Clent, where in the early 1930s **Sunfield Children's Home** had been established, the first Rudolf Steiner Curative Education Centre in England. The impulse for this venture in Stourbridge came after a group of 'Bottoners' had asked several years earlier for a more independent urban-based life in a community supportive setting. Thus the first Camphill community in a town setting came into being in 1969 in Stourbridge, where there was also a Rudolf Steiner school, Christian church and the nearby biodynamic Broome Farm. It took only six weeks for all the newcomers to find jobs locally.

England's first Training Centre and Adolescent College started in **The Mount** in rural Sussex in 1971, using an old monastery building. It began a unique series of communities

Peter Bergel, Tourmaline, Botton village

for young people perhaps too old for schools and too young for the adult village communities. Also in 1971 a remarkable social policy conference took place at Botton Village, looking at adult provision now that the closing of the workhouse/mental hospital institutions was gathering pace. It confirmed the supportive environment places like Camphill offered.

Camphill in England and Wales, as in other countries with an institutionalized provision for people with special needs, had shown the way to a unique alternative, drawing on Rudolf Steiner's Fundamental Social Law to create social, economic and cultural settings for all people, including those with special needs. It was a good time for Camphill communities, attracting both a younger generation of co-workers, and people with special needs now coming from social services and local authority placements, and so growth and development of the communities continued apace. What present day Camphill has to contend with is the 'glorious' history that Camphill has had in places like England and Wales. That is not meant in a self-gratifying way, but when contrasted with the difficult history of social provision

Farm workers, Botton village

in English and Welsh institutions, where there was lack of choice and the exclusion of people with learning disabilities from meaningful engagement in society, Camphill pioneered inclusion in sheltered community environments.

In the seventies and eighties Camphill in England and Wales saw the extension of the adult community idea. In Malton in 1974 a group from Lions International bought and provided **The Croft House** and garden for a group of young co-workers from Botton to set up the second urban community for Camphill in this Yorkshire market town.

The Sheiling Thornbury developed its own training centre at **The Hatch** and in a radical move, also from Thornbury, a college was established in mid-Wales, called **Coleg Elidyr**. This arose with active support from parents, a reflection of an original idea of Dr König that parents should be more involved in the communities. It tried to work with the parents and friends groups and, as a result, The Ring came into existence to provide Camphill with financial, social and spiritual support. This happened firstly through fundraising and social support, then through the parents' gradual understanding of the deeper concepts of Rudolf Steiner's anthroposophy, thereby accompanying the core values of the communities' life and work.

Interest in self-sufficiency for Camphill brought about **Oaklands Park** in 1978, near The Grange in Gloucestershire, with the vision that the produce from the land should support the community. The first project in the north-west brought about the community of **Garthwaite** in 1974, to support children going to the local special school in Kendal. This was sold several years later, making available money to begin **Camphill Pennine Community** near Wakefield, thus carrying on the training centre stream in the north of England. In the late sixties a project to develop a small school and vicarage in the Shropshire village of Chelmarsh, called **St Peter's**, became an important project in an isolated rural community. When it ceased, money from the sale went to develop **The Mount Community**.

By 1981 the New Education Act for England and Wales recognized that all children irrespective of ability should receive an education up to school-leaving age. There was already the Camphill Schools Seminar in Ringwood and Thornbury, but now the first of a number of training courses began, such as the Youth Guidance Seminar, tailored to the needs of colleges. This ushered in a time of distance learning with several weekend courses culminating in a diploma project. Introduction courses and Year

Two programmes all started to formalize at this time. It's interesting to note on another level that due to high unemployment and lack of apprenticeships at the time, government sponsored Job Creation Schemes started to help Camphill communities with essential maintenance and building programmes.

Requests for Camphill's way of community life now started coming from local authorities, notably the Milton Keynes Development Corporation and Middlesbrough Borough Council, and so two urban communities came into existence as a result in the mid eighties. **Milton Keynes** and **Larchfield Community** were both a fulfilment of the ideals of the Camphill pioneers: to be asked to come to places where a need could be demonstrated. In the case of Milton Keynes it was to build a community in a new town, and in the case of Middlesbrough it was to create work opportunities in an area affected by high unemployment. The Middlesbrough project had come about as a result of the 1981 International Year of The Disabled and a visit by officers of Middlesborough Council. This in a real sense was a meaningful and fulfilling testament to the Camphill pioneers.

Meanwhile another request from a small group of anthroposophists and friends in Devon led to the idea of a village community in the county, greatly encouraged by the huge number of mental hospital closures and the urgent need for sheltered accommodation for their residents. **Hapstead Village** near Buckfastleigh came about officially on December 31,1979. A request from an East Anglian landowner with a son at The Sheiling School brought about **Thornage Hall**, a training and adult community in rolling countryside near Holt in North Norfolk, with a focus on special education and community building in an otherwise isolated rural community.

Local authorities were one avenue of founding a community. Ideals of how to work together with a special ideal was another approach. Thus through the Arts and Crafts Movement, inspirations from such figures as William Morris brought about the ideal that beautifully made items in craft workshops could be the domain of young people with special needs. Thus **William Morris House**, near Stonehouse on the Stroud canal in Gloucestershire, came about. Taking the crafts into the wider community where a modern visitor centre complete with coffee bar, shops and workshops led to the establishment of **Taurus Crafts**. With easy access off the newly completed Lydney bypass roundabout, visitors flocked to this modern interpretation of a Camphill centre.

From crafts to the craft of giving people with specific needs a supportive environment.

So with **Camphill St Albans** came an independent living community in the famous cathedral city north of London for those with mental health needs. Whilst for those growing older and needing a supportive urban environment, **Gannicox Camphill Community** in Stroud came into being at the start of the 21st century, where residents of all ages can access college, adult education and retail services.

Camphill England and Wales in the nineties and into the new millenium has developed not so much in physical new communities but rather in forms, meeting spaces and ways to respond to a raft of changes that affect the social providers in a country which has seen, in twenty years, root and branch changes to the way the person with special needs is approached, treated and regarded in society. And it reflects a new generation of Camphill's personnel and how it wishes to live in community.

This could be characterized as a change from a group sense to an individual approach. From wholesale provision with an emphasis

Dairy worker, Botton village

on physical surroundings and fire protection, as outlined in the 1984 Registered Homes Act, to individually based assessment of needs, choice, inclusion and opportunity, as seen in the Supporting People Legislation of 2003. This has meant for Camphill a move from the more working environment to increased college provision, training for life, and in some cases a move to achievement in sport and adult education, taking opportunities to organize conferences and the dreaming of dreams. What was once hardly thought about for people with special needs is now a possibility: ballooning, horse riding, organizing events, or saying what is going to happen in groups. England as a country has played an important part in these developments with a Camphill family and friends group sponsoring a 'person-centred planning' project with Lottery funding, no less. In the school communities, legislation to protect vulnerable children has led to a complete reappraisal of the place and care of the child with special needs, creating the philosophy of a 'child-centred environment.'

How Camphill has worked with these developments could be the subject of a book, for the individual and his or her relationship to community is an important issue. For an individual to ask to be excluded from the Festival Play, Bible Evening or communal gathering is sometimes painful for a community, however much it wants to support, care and allow the individual to develop.

Much discussion group work and deliberation has happened to try and give new emphasis to the individual needs through 'Speak-up groups', 'symposiums' and 'getting together conferences' and a Social Worker Support Group has come about, honouring the wish to be part of a community. Indeed, the latest legislation, which brings in individual budgets for people with learning disabilities, gives a clear choice for the individual and thereby a healthy decision can be made to live in an intentional community. In making that informed choice, both the community and the individual person are recognized. For the co-worker population, new proposals towards a Curative Education and Social Therapy degree course, plus official recognition of all the communities' introduction courses, are in the pipeline with the help of the Crossfields Institute and University of Western England.

Accompanying these developments comes the question of how the modern community is structured, the work of governance leading from health and safety to risk-assessment issues. This creates the picture of the building of an organization first and then allowing a community to grow out of this, rather than the previous tendency of the other way around. This is the modern approach and in some Camphill communities in England and Wales managers have been appointed to help with organizational tasks in places like Camphill Devon, Oaklands Park, Thornage, Milton Keynes, Ringwood and Thornbury. First impressions of these managerial approaches are very much associated with the type of community and the particular need for such a person. This could be to build a new group of community supported and employed co-workers after a complete change of staff as retirement, and new life situations emerge for the long-term carrying group. New regulations which call for highly technical knowledge of the social policy approach call forth a new generation of carrying people.

Suffice to say that the technical work, spiritual work and the human work of community and its organization have been challenged as never before. These managers, after some very steep learning curves getting to know the Camphill communities they have become involved in, remarked after an important meeting held in the summer of 2009 how remarkable the communities they have come to manage are.

Baker in the changing room, Botton village

The Irish region

NEIL MACLEAN, MISCHA FEKETE AND
HETTY V. BRANDENBURG

Ireland, the Emerald Isle, land of saints and scholars, Ireland of the welcomes, the ancient home of the Celtic civilization, is the beautiful green island where Christianity has flourished for many centuries. Ireland, previously the most underdeveloped country in western Europe, has undergone a huge transformation in recent years, going through boom to almost bust. The conflict in Northern Ireland is now on the way to being resolved through the commitment of many people to a political process.

Curative education, the village impulse, and biodynamic agriculture are streams meandering through Ireland, wanting to bring healing. Camphill North and South, formerly very closely linked and one Camphill region, have diverged considerably under the different state administrations, although on the human, cultural and spiritual level there is still much to connect us.

Development in Northern Ireland has proceeded mainly within three large communities. **Glencraig** was the first of these centres, which was founded after Dr König met with parents and friends of children with learning difficulties in Belfast in 1953. It continues to be the largest community, with children, teenagers and adults in separate houses, and one house with elderly people. It has more than two hundred people, a complex internal structure, a biodynamic farm and garden, craft and service workshops, the hall and a medical-therapy building. Glencraig is host to the Curative Education and Social Therapy Seminar, which in future will continue as the Camphill Northern Ireland Seminar. Recently demands from the department of education, the dogma of mainstreaming, and applications of fewer children with ever more complex needs have changed many aspects of the community. It has become essential to address issues around professionalism, documentation and qualifications.

Day pupils, external staff and a community of former co-workers and others associated with Glencraig have built up a rich support network for Glencraig and other anthroposophical ventures in the neighbourhood of Holywood, which also has a Christian Community centre and a Steiner school.

In 1971 the expanding need for adult places led to the foundation of the **Mourne Grange Village Community** near Kilkeel, on the south-eastern shore of Northern Ireland. Lying between the sea and the imposing majestic Mountains of Mourne, Mourne Grange set out to be a village devoted to working and caring for the land. Crafts, arts and therapeutic activity are well established, alongside biodynamic agriculture, which has remained of central importance since the beginning of the community.

It has a beautiful spacious hall, which hosts a rich cultural life, including the Mourne Grange Ceili Band. The coffee and craft shop and the health-food store attract many customers. There is a Waldorf kindergarten and a small Waldorf school, which helps young families to find their way to the community. Mourne Grange has a relatively high number of ageing people, and has consciously taken on board their well-being, which has led to the development of the Helios Health Centre.

In spite of the rapid development of Mourne Grange, there was still a demand for more places for adults, and in 1984, Camphill acquired a farm at **Clanabogan** in County Tyrone. Clanabogan was the first step to the west. The ground had been well prepared and Clanabogan soon established itself as a small, land-working village with a lot of land and a strong biodynamic agriculture impulse, as well as a Waldorf playgroup with children from the locality. This non-denominational caring work brought an element of healing to the surrounding community. An Introductory Biodynamic Seminar has been initiated here, which is open to Camphill and other interested people. Pioneering renewable energy projects have brought many people into the community, including groups of students from the South West College in Omagh.

Camphill Holywood, an inspiring urban development, began in 1996 in a closed-down bakery. This urban community radiates the Camphill impulse into the town, and provides work for disadvantaged adults. There is an organic food shop, bakery and café, which have won many awards for high quality food. Recently it has also added an urban house community. They have found creative ways to include the local population in their festival celebrations, and are hoping to develop further as a town community.

Within the Irish Republic growth has followed the country's fortunes. Beginning with **Duffcarrig** in 1972, when Dublin parents of children at Glencraig found a house on a small farm in County Wexford on the east coast, and the first group moved there from Glencraig in February 1972. The republic was the poorer country, but the new community received enthusiastic and generous support from both government and the people. Perhaps the fact that caring for people with learning difficulties and the deprived has traditionally been the responsibility of the religious orders gave the Camphill community approach a special significance. The work of Camphill quickly found a home in the south.

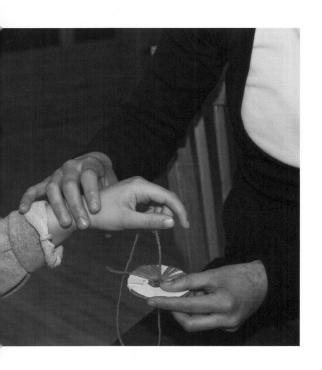

After a period of expansion and consolidation the call came to take up new tasks. A group of parents with autistic children in Dublin asked Camphill to start a school for difficult and disturbed children. In 1979 **Ballytobin** in County Kilkenny, a small farm which grew to become a home and school for children with learning difficulties, was started. Like Glencraig, Ballytobin also included a number of adults with special needs.

With Ballytobin becoming firmly established there again arose the need for more adult places in the south. For several years the supporters of Camphill had hoped for a development around Dublin, the country's capital, and in 1985 a community was founded at **Dunshane**, near Naas in County Kildare, not far from Dublin. Dunshane took up the task of training adolescents and young adults for mature adulthood, but has transformed in more recent years into an adult community.

A very different process led to the creation of another community. A group of people in a parish near Ballytobin asked whether it would be possible to start a home for adults with learning difficulties in their area. Discussions on how best to do this took place over several years, and local people searched for a suitable home for this work. Late in 1986 a 38-acre farm at **Temple Michael**, Grangemockler, in County Tipperary, was bought and the house renovated for occupation late in 1988. This was the first facility for adults with special needs in the whole of South Tipperary, and stands as an expression of social concern and commitment of the rural community at Grangemockler.

As the Ballytobin children grew towards adulthood, there was a long search for a suitable place to create a sister community nearby. In 1987 a small farm was purchased at **Kyle**, three miles away, where children who grew up in Ballytobin and others have made their adult home.

Meanwhile Camphill in the South Kilkenny area developed in a unique fashion, with the forming of a network of smaller communities, each having its own purpose and character. This process has led to much growth in the South Kilkenny and South Tipperary region, which has resulted in the 'community of communities,' a network of Ballytobin and six adult communities and a non-residential journeyman young adult training initiative. These communities, though independent economically, remain in close cooperation on the cultural, community and spiritual level. This was a deliberate step rather than following the traditional large community, and has proved very successful.

The early nineties saw much growth and enthusiasm, which was accompanied by many new people committing to Camphill. The need from several people in Duffcarrig to explore new steps in their life and the offer of an old barn in **Jerpoint** gave birth to a new community near Thomastown. A new impulse of outreach at around the same time led to the establishing of new urban communities. An offshoot of Dunshane in Kilcullen brought about the **Bridge Community**, with a coffee shop also selling books and crafts to the wider community. Likewise in Thomastown the offering of a gift of a beautiful urban garden led to a similar shop called the **Watergarden**, which soon drew a community to form around it.

The donation of a piece of land in County Monaghan soon helped Camphill to expand beyond Leinster and the south-east of Ireland in forming a small rural community close to **Ballybay**, just south of the border to Northern Ireland.

It was the mid nineties and Ireland at this time was slowly changing. It was becoming less insular and more secular. Camphill started to become more part of the world at large. The concept of social entrepreneurship became a driving force for new impulses, not directly connected to care.

Ballytobin became host to a biogas plant. This alternative energy venture does not only provide a safe way for farmers to dispose of surplus slurry in an environmentally friendly manner and receive a storable concentrated natural fertilizer in return, but also creates heat and electricity for the use of the community and compost for the gardens. It is now a business that adds another layer of social interaction with the wider community.

A further urban community established itself in **Carrick-on-Suir** around the same time.

Ireland at this time experienced a period of unprecedented growth, a phenomenon which came to be known as the Celtic Tiger. The increase in individualism was also experienced in Camphill as an increasing social force, and this led to several communities, such as Thomastown and Carrick-on Suir creating new forms of independent living. The **Journeyman Programme**, a new non-residential training facility for school leavers, initially from Ballytobin, started around this time.

The recognition of the creative potential of each individual has always been a cornerstone of Camphill. The attempt to facilitate a budding artist by the name of George McCutcheon in Ballytobin initiated a unique facility in Callan, County Kilkenny. **Kilkenny Collective for Arts Talent** has meanwhile developed into a centre that offers art and design courses, evening classes and summer courses for local people, co-workers and people with special needs. It also houses a permanent studio for people with special needs whoare exploring their artistic vocation.

The recognition of the importance of art as a social force saw the building of many beautiful halls over the years (notably in Mourne Grange in the north and several others in the south). Castalia Hall in Ballytobin deserves a special mention. This magnificent Byzantine style hall was built around oaken pillars, and attracts internationally acclaimed musicians for regular concert performances open to the public. It currently houses the Kilkenny Music Society's Steinway piano.

Musically Camphill's artistic creativity culminated in The Celtic Lyre Orchestra, a group of over fifty musicians of all abilities, from communities in both the north and south of Ireland, which performed to a full house in the National Concert Hall in Dublin in 2002, attended by the president of Ireland, Mary McAleese.

Callan is another urban development, partly in an old workhouse, where some three thousand souls perished during the great famine of the nineteenth century. In collaboration with

Kilkenny County Council, Camphill is renovating the derelict and protected structure, with plans for a local health centre in one part, incorporating C.E.A.R.T., a Camphill inspired alternative therapy centre. Unfortunately the present financial crisis affecting all government bodies in Ireland has resulted in the delay or withholding of funds promised for this and many other Camphill initiatives.

Camphill in Callan also works in close collaboration with the **L'Arche Community**, in the realm of work and culture. Together with another life-sharing initiative called Kings River Community we have united to form the Life-sharing Alliance, a valuable support when dealing with authorities.

In 2002 and 2003 Ireland was rocked by revelations of institutional abuse in religious institutions, many of these looking after people with special needs. Society was shocked by the extent and longevity of these insidious goings-on and demanded accountability and regulatory frameworks. The state embarked on a complete review of best practice in the area of disability services. The National Disability Authority requested submissions regarding developing standards from all stakeholders and Camphill participated actively in this debate, where it clearly has much to offer from decades of experience in the field of living with people with learning disabilities. This was finally recognized when HIQA (Health Information and Quality Authority) offered Camphill membership of the Life-sharing Alliance representation on its standards advisory group.

Needs, opportunities, individualism and the availability of funding over the last decade led to more growth. Land purchased in **Dingle** four years earlier finally became another Camphill community. Initiatives in County Clare near a thriving Steiner school came to some fruition, and the East Clare initiative gradually grew into **Camphill Community Mountshannon**. The use of a large suburban house no longer in use by a religious order gave rise to **Camphill Community Greenacres**, which now, no longer utilizing the old house, is spread through housing estates in the same vicinity in three ordinary houses.

Duffcarrig, the oldest community in the republic has been trying to reach out over the years. Finally **Camphill Ballymoney** came into being a short distance away, with intentions for a shop and tearoom, within walking distance of the parent community.

The Bridge Community's desire for more farmland during expensive boom times led to the purchase of **Grangebeg**. Situated on a hillside with beautiful views, available money led to rapid development of two house communities, a hall and farm buildings. There was always a desire for a third community in the vicinity, and its geographical position has led it to become part of a triangle with The Bridge and Dunshane.

Pioneering and building communities is one thing, maintaining and living in communities is another, and several communities in Ireland are challenged from lack of dedicated committed Camphillers. Increased regulation, different standards and changing times are putting Ireland under similar pressures to other countries and stimulating us to think of creative solutions.

That the Camphill spirit can triumph, in particular through the arts, when individuals, together with others, put their will at the disposal of a higher aim, seems tangible on this emerald isle, the land of ancient bards and scholars, where community has always been a feature of life.

The Central European region

RICHARD STEEL

The history of the Central European region

Above and below: Lehenhof

As in the United States and South Africa, Camphill's work in Central Europe began in the fifties. The Camphill impulse, which had its roots in Austria, Silesia and Switzerland returned again to the area that had been the centre of destruction and the cause of König's exile. Through many consultations and requests by parents, the demand for Camphill in Germany had become apparent. Dr König was also especially keen to bring the ideas of Camphill to fruition in Germany, as these ideals had always been linked to the destiny or potential of Central Europe. Curative work had begun in **Christophorus**, Holland, in 1954 and links had been made to the Irish region, from where Dr Hans-Heinrich Engel assisted to create a music-therapy training course. In 1958 a small group of co-workers from Scotland started in **Brachenreuthe** near Überlingen on Lake Constance to work with severely handicapped, cerebral palsied and speech-impaired children.

Karl König visited regularly, and then took up residence in Brachenreuthe in 1964 together with Alix Roth, his secretary and assistant. König experienced the activity related to old Central European spirituality: the early Christianizing of the landscape through the devout work of Celtic monks and the influence of the medieval mystics. In addition to curative education, the husbandry of the earth and land was a central impulse of Camphill at Lake Constance. Dr Eberhard Schickler, a professional colleague of Dr König, helped to inaugurate Camphill's work in Germany.

Brachenreuthe, once described as the Camphill Movement's dearest child, was deeply influenced by Karl König's charismatic and powerful personality. Requests for admission grew dramatically, and a second centre soon became necessary. A new residential school, **Föhrenbühl**, was founded nearby, and in 1966 another in **Bruckfelden**. Positive contacts with colleagues in the wider curative education movement were soon established.

With the expanding school work the need became clear to start a village community for school leavers and to accommodate the increasing admission requests for adults in need of special care. Government and local authorities were open to new developments. After a first attempt at the farm in Brachenreuthe the village idea took root at the **Lehenhof**, an estate nearby, in 1964. The official opening fell on Karl König's last earthly birthday, in September 1965.

As the Camphill Movement grew, it was formed into regional groupings. Together with a council of delegates, Karl König assumed responsibility for the different centres within the Central European region. The co-workers of **Aigues-Vertes** and **St Prex**, two places in Switzerland on Lake Geneva, had asked to join, the Camphill Movement. Thus, to begin with, the newly-founded region was centred round the lakes of Constance and Geneva.

Until König's death in March 1966 the curative educational and medical therapeutic impulses were firmly rooted within the schools. The village idea had also come to realization, relating curative education with agricultural work and new social forms of living together in community.

During these first years, four pillars of residential curative educational work were formed and established: therapeutic efforts for the individual child; the educational work of the teachers' college and the area of schooling; the daily care of children within their residential house communities; and thorough medical supervision. During this time care for movement-disturbed, speech-impaired and autistic children was the primary focus.

Linking on to his work in the east before the war, Karl König made plans to visit East Germany, Hungary and Czechoslovakia, as Camphill was sought for in Eastern Europe. However, he died before this could happen.

At first the Central European region developed more in the west. **Christophorus**, the centre in Zeist, Holland, became part of the region; in 1973 **Humanus Haus** was opened near Berne, Switzerland, geographically in the central point between the two lakes of Geneva and Constance; in the same year the **Karl König School in Nürnberg** became the first non-residential Camphill school, and in 1975 **Thomas House** was established in Berlin, caring for pre-school children. In 1976 the fifth centre at Lake Constance began through the initiative of parents in Föhrenbühl; **Hermannsberg** was to be the second village community there, and in Vienna, Austria, an association was

Above and below: Lehenhof

formed which, a year later, began to build a village community in **Liebenfels**, Carinthia. In 1977 the first Camphill community in France, **Le Béal**, was founded in Provence; in 1980 a small land-based community **Het Maartenhuis** on the island of Texel extended the tasks in Holland to include social therapeutic work, and in 1987 the **Hausenhof Village Community** was established in close collaboration with the Karl König school at Nürnberg, Germany.

From the early seventies co-workers met annually to help ensure that the region stayed 'alive and vital.' These meetings focussed often on Rudolf Steiner's ideas concerning renewal of the social organism (the threefold social order) as well as its implications for the various Camphill communities. Out of the intensive phase of the seventies three different councils were formed to consider human concerns and legal matters, the formation of cooperative associations in the economic sphere and cultural (or spiritual) life. These three councils superseded the original council of delegates and lead to a new regional grouping and to the founding of an annual regional 'forum.' Many of the questions dealt with related to the development of social structures within the modern political and economic setting: the more idealistic aspects of community living and cooperation on many levels within the region.

Simultaneously Camphill's relationship to other curative education schools and villages in Central Europe developed in such a way that in 1979 the Conference of Curative Education, Social Therapy and Social Work was established at the Goetheanum in Dornach, Switzerland. The regional structures within the individual countries also complimented this common ground.

With the opening of Eastern Europe in 1989, the Central European region was constantly challenged by very new needs coming from the eastern countries. Karl König had many contacts since pre-war times and hoped that something would evolve there. It became a conscious task over many years to be aware of friends in those countries, to support them where possible and to keep them and the specific qualities of the Eastern European people in mind. At the same time three village communities developed out of parents' initiatives: in the Pfalz, **Königsmühle**; in Berlin, **Alt-Schönow**, and **Sellen** close to Münster, towards the Dutch border. The **Markus-Gemeinschaft** in Hauteroda,

Thüringen, had managed to survive as an anthroposophic institution throughout the previous twenty years of the East German regime and could officially become Camphill in the early nineties, as was the case for the small family initiative in the south of Poland, **Wójtówka**. After the turn of the millennium the village communities in the Czech Republic, **Česke Kópisty**, and in Hungary, **Camphill Vellem**, could begin. As from 2006 the region connected six language areas (without counting Swiss and Austrian German!).

Germany

The curative educational and social-therapeutic work of Camphill in Germany started in **Brachenreuthe**. Now it is a community with children from kindergarten age right through school life, including a training centre for learning crafts. An outreach with an early intervention programme, **Föhrenbühl**, twenty kilometres away now has ten house communities with around one hundred children and adolescents and about twenty day pupils. The nursery class has been integrative since 1974 and now includes a growing group of toddlers. There is a well-established training school for youngsters that has ten craft areas as well as classroom work.

Opposite page and this page: Images from Hermannsberg

Adalbert Stifter House, near Bruckfelden and between Brachenreuthe and Föhrenbühl, was opened by Karl König in early 1966, so that Dr Hans and Susanne Müller-Wiedemann could begin work with autistic children. Since then it has become a training centre for youngsters and includes a special unit for some with very particular needs. As it now legally belongs to the same school institute as Brachenreuthe and Föhrenbühl and has been extended over the years to incorporate five houses and the trainee building, it is now called **Camphill Schulgemeinschaft Bruckfelden**.

The village communities **Lehenhof** and **Hermannsberg** are well-established settlements with their own workshop structure, which has been formed into a limited company in its own rights. Both villages have extensive garden and farming facilities with apprentice placements and have developed care units for the elderly, which had become a strong need through the ageing of the community and its inhabitants. Lehenhof has expanded with a number of house communities into the neighbouring municipalities. The two village communities have also begun cooperating with the Camphill schools and other institutions close by to create sheltered living possibilities and work situations that are more strongly integrated into the town of Überlingen. This initiative is known as **S**ozial **K**ulturelle **I**ntegrations **D**ienst.

The Camphill centres at Lake Constance have together created a separate company to run the adult training course for curative education and social therapy, which now has full state recognition. The Camphill Seminar therefore has its own building in the local village of Frickingen.

In 1973, work with pre-school children began in Nürnberg. This grew into a nursery school in 1975, and then became the **Karl König School**, the first day centre in the Camphill Movement. From the start, a very fruitful cooperation with parents ensured the growth of the school. Now the growing school with craft training has extended to a nearby location, where the **Camphill Werkstatt am Goldbach** offers day placements for work in various areas to about forty adults.

Following the untiring efforts of co-workers, parents and friends of the Nürnberg School, the ancient and isolated **Hausenhof** farmhouse sixty kilometres west of the city, was bought in 1983, and in 1985 biodynamic farming started. The Hausenhof Village Community offers a home and work to over sixty people.

The name Camphill came to Berlin in 1975 when a psychiatric-neurological consultant wished to relate to the curative educational and social impulses of Camphill. Supported by parents, a day centre for speech-impaired pre-school children was founded. In this centre, **Thomas House** for Curative Education and Speech Therapy, a wide range of therapies are offered for about 45 young children. Regular in-service courses are held there. The residential centre for adults, **Alt-Schönow** has 45 placements and most of the adults there work in a nearby sheltered workshop. Both centres are on the outskirts of the city.

Opposite page and below: images from Hermannsberg

The village community of Sellen

The **Camphill Lebensgemeinschaft Königsmühle** is also on the edge of town, near to Neustadt, Pfalz and is well integrated there into the larger community. It used to be a well-known spa hotel and the old tradition is still accepted that they open their coffee shop to hikers and visitors. There, 21 adults find a home and work. The village community of **Sellen** is mainly land-based but has housing, a shop and café within the local town too. Also the impressive workshop building is on the main road just out of town. Altogether sixty residents are there. They are geographically closer to the Dutch centres than to any of their German neighbours.

Raffael House, Sellen

Martin House, Sellen

Markus Gemeinschaft in Hauteroda has had a special background through its very existence during the communist era, but also many innovative steps have been taken within this ecologically and economically exploited landscape. The task in such an environment is a curative one for society, as Karl König had pointed out, which not only brings success but has in addition other advantages. The community is also well known for its social initiatives, giving work opportunities for many people, including the local population. The five existing houses, workshops, the farm and also the new buildings are scattered around the parish of Hauteroda. The farm is extensive, working together with neighbours and running a modern productive dairy; vocational chances are not only offered for care work but also in food processing and the kitchen, which delivers food to a number of institutions in the wider area; new concepts for communal energy projects, for care of the elderly and with micro-credit banking link the community to its immediate and wider surroundings. A high quality youth hostel is run there which provides the basis also for many schools and work-groups.

Below: Shop and café, Sellen

France

Le Béal Community near the Rhône began in 1977 following a request from a family farming with handicapped people who wished to pass on their responsibility. In the midst of Provence, influenced by the Mediterranean climate, with the air enriched by the scent of many herbs, and imbued with the light that inspired Cézanne and Van Gogh, the community began its work in a large house. During the French Revolution silk was produced there. Le Béal is recognized by the French authorities as providing new social forms of living and working with people in need of special care. Work on the land and care for plants, shrubs and trees form the core of the work for the community. The small community relates strongly to its environment and is known for its food products but also through it cultural activity.

Above: Produce for sale, Le Béal
Below: Jam-making, Le Béal

Below: Perceval

Holland

Christophorus in Zeist, in the middle of Holland, was founded in 1953. In February that year there was a heavy flood, a terrifying event, as much of the country lies below sea level, and the founding group had witnessed the way people helped each other. This group formed a committee called the League for Social, Pedagogical and Therapeutic Impulses. They started by opening a house to care for maladjusted children, and later other houses were acquired, forming an urban community within the larger community. From the beginning the co-workers worked to transform the sandy soil by planting trees and cultivating gardens.

Today, there are one hundred children and young people there who go to a local school, which has a special Waldorf department. For the young adults there are workshops on the estate. Good relations have been established with the other curative homes and close cooperation with the other institutions. In fact legally Christophorus has now merged with a local care organization, called Amerpoort, which now encompasses conventional services and the specialized anthroposophical approach of Christophorus. This organization also provides workshop places in the next town of Amersfoort and in connection with this Christophorus has been developing housing for adults since 2004 in the suburban area. At the moment 23 young adults have been taken in.

Immediately behind the sand dunes on the island of Texel **Het Maartenhuis** is a small centre, which is very involved in the cultural life of the island. The village community houses thirty adults and two children with special needs but offers another sixty work opportunities during the day. In 1994 the **Orion Community** was founded within the outskirts of the city of Rotterdam. 91 adults and twelve children live there together in fifteen houses scattered around the suburb called Zevenkamp. The community centre is offered for use and used often by artists living in the neighbourhood for their exhibitions. It is an ideal for the community to be a meeting place of various cultures and peoples. Their own cultural activities are also open for the public.

In 1981 a small land-oriented community was founded in the north of Holland, **De Norderhoeve** in Schoorl, where the North Holland Dune Nature Park begins. The community joined the Camphill Movement in 1997. A varied group of people work on this farming project together; they are adults with a history of substance abuse, with various psychiatric problems, some people with burn-out and adults with learning disabilities. Mutual aid, support and enrichment are direct results of this community endeavour. The flowing together of social work, the therapeutic and medical work, education and cultural activity is an important focus of this farming settlement.

Camphill GezinsKring 't Huys was founded in 2002 in Houten, central Holland. Children are admitted that have been removed from their parents through legal proceedings. In these cases the disabilities or disfunctionality of the families are the reasons for taking in the children, not their own special needs. But these children have of course usually suffered the damaging effects that come from unstable and unsafe situations, and for this reason they need an environment that offers them special care.

Switzerland

Just above the small town of St Prex on Lake Geneva, 22 kilometres west of Lausanne, and surrounded by vineyards, is the **Centre de Pédagogie Curative Perceval**. This Camphill community has expanded from an organization offering a residential special school to one that also provides living and working opportunities for handicapped adults. With the building of two large care houses in 2006 it now also takes in a large number of children with severe multiple handicaps. Altogether 113 children, youngsters and adults are looked after. Apart from an integrative kindergarten, school and training centre with crafts and workshops, three of the houses for adults are within neighbouring towns, including a shop which sells community produce as well as newspapers and general goods.

The village community of Aigues Vertes withdrew from the Camphill Movement in 1995 after a long process of questioning with the board members, leaving Perceval and Le Béal, which are 370 kilometres from each other and in different countries, to be the only French-speaking centres.

The impulse which led to the founding of **Humanus House** grew out of experiences gained in curative education work at Perceval. Humanus House started in 1973 within a farming area near Berne about halfway between Lake Geneva and Lake Constance. The community now offers a social and working life for over eighty handicapped people and a further twenty come in on a daily basis. Apart from the twelve family houses, workshops

Below: Perceval

and swimming centre there is a nearby farm and also a factory for Choroi musical instruments in the town of Langenthal. For the main group of youngsters craft training and schooling prepare them for integration into society. Another group that trained there stays on living and working there in diverse work areas. Some of these workshops, along with the garden and farm, offer professional training. There is also an adult education course for social work on various diploma levels there. Many conferences and cultural activities take place in the hall and the café and craft shop on the main road is open to the public.

Left: Humanus House
Below: Perceval

Above left: the swimming pool at Humanus House
Above and below: Humanus House

Austria

Austria is the birthplace of anthroposophy, and also of Camphill in a sense, but it had to wait until 1976 for the establishment of its first Camphill endeavour. One may wonder why it took so long for Camphill to find its way back to its homeland, having been established for so long in other countries. Perhaps this shows that the Camphill Movement, although of Central European origin, is independent of geographical and national boundaries and can find a home in any country where it's needed.

Camphill **Liebenfels** is about 25 kilometres north of Klagenfurt in the beautiful and harmonious landscape of the Carinthian heartland, not far from the borders of Slovenia and Italy.

Liebenfels comprises three settlements, Wertsch, Mossenig and Pflausach, spread out with from two to seven kilometres between them. The six households are in converted farmhouses and two newly built houses in Pflausach, which is the only estate owned, the other two places being rented. Pflausach is most beautifully situated at a height of 850 metres with a splendid view over the valley below and the Karawanken Mountains of Slovenia.

A simple but lovely assembly hall seating 120 has been built at Pflausach in a converted outbuilding. Quite a variety of cultural activities take place there, and they are increasingly attracting a growing number of visitors from the surrounding area.

The Austrian character has no doubt influenced the way of life in Liebenfels, and given it a certain colouring. Yet in the large family of Camphill centres, Liebenfels has found a place and endeavours to make its contribution.

Poland

The small community in the south of Poland is right on the Czech border in Silesia. It began as a family initiative during the communist regime and joined the Camphill Movement in 1996. Since then a lot has been done to develop the property, with a new house being built and a farm in the first stage of development. In 2001 a small workshop building was added to offer occupational possibilities other than the garden and farm, and a holiday cottage is run for visitors and tourists. The official establishment of work places has also meant that apart from their own fourteen residents, other people in need of sheltered work come in from the surrounding area.

Opposite page and below:
images from Austria

Top: Vegetable harvesting, Česke Kópisty
Bottom: Drying maize

Czech Republic

An association was founded in 1998 to prepare the ground for Camphill in the Czech Republic. In 2001 the property was signed over and a start was made to renovate buildings so that social therapy could begin. Most of the work was done by the initiating group itself, using only the donations they could get. The group of buildings are in the village of **Česke Kópisty**, sixty kilometres north-west of Prague, directly on the banks of the Elbe (called 'Labe' in Czech). The land there is very fertile and it's known as 'the garden of Bohemia,' but the small village belongs to the greater municipality of Theresienstadt, which is steeped in history, the latter part extremely negative as it was one of the famous Jewish ghettos and collecting place before deportation, for instance to Auschwitz. So there is a lot of destiny to be balanced out. In 2005 the building work had progressed well enough to start day care and work in a weavery, and fourteen acres of good land was bought directly on the riverside. Soon they were able to sell biodynamic vegetables regularly in Prague. In January of 2005 the first group of residents could move in. Now six adults are looked after there and five come in on a daily basis.

Hungary

After intensive preparations a start was made in 2007 with curative education in the Camphill village **Velem**, near Szombathelmy, in connection with the Waldorf school there. A new house was built onto the large former children's home on this wonderful estate in the hills on the West Hungarian border with Austria. An attempt was started to run the community and school by free financing and without state aid, to prevent state intervention.

Top: Co-worker and residents
Bottom: Velem, one month after opening

General outlook

Within the past few years, the centres in Germany, France, Holland, Austria and Switzerland in particular have made efforts to relate more directly to their surroundings, and to seek cooperation with other endeavours. One of the main preoccupations at present is the question of management structure and procedure needing on the one hand to comply with complex administrative and financial legislation, and on the other to recognize values and ideals that need to be upheld and developed within the rapidly changing social environment. In the pioneering phase of the eastern parts of the region, the Czech Republic, Hungary and Poland, the questions are more basic, within the context of political, economic and cultural turmoil following the collapse of the communist regimes. During this time there have been great efforts within the region to assist with the dire necessities in those countries, and it is important to remember, for instance, the intensive aid given, particularly through the Swiss communities headed by Hans Spalinger, to initiatives in Romania. This brought about the organization of eleven centres around the country; the original ones being still affiliated with Camphill: **Simeria**, near to Buckarest, where 120 children and adults live and attend school, kindergarten, workshops and therapies, and a further 37 youngsters live and work together doing farm and workshop activities. In the south there is a village community at **Urlati** with fifty youngsters and adults in social therapeutic care.

This engagement in the eastern parts of Europe has been important for the regional process in a time of questioning the relevance and future prospects of Camphill work within the western established democracies.

A step much further to the east was made in 2009 when, after years of preparation, a therapeutic community could officially be opened in Vietnam: **The Peaceful Bamboo Family** in Hue. Due to the longstanding efforts of Lissie and Tho Ha Vinh and the training of Vietnamese co-workers in Perceval, the Camphill centres in the French language area have led the region to 'adopt' this initiative for its initial phase.

The Northern European region

LUDWIG KRAUS

During the last twenty years, the character of the Camphill Movement in the Northern European region has undergone some deep changes. Over many years cooperation between the villages in Norway, Sweden and Finland formed a north-western constellation. In the nineties communities in Latvia, Estonia and Russia were established, a geographical expansion to the east across the Baltic. This was followed by a community in southern Sweden, a gesture towards Central Europe. Afterwards there were a number of social initiatives, hoping to link into the Camphill Movement, that stretched over central Russia to the Urals and the Ukraine. A different dimension opened which expressed itself in new polarities, not only geographical. This development brought qualities and tasks to the region that required new perspectives and purposes.

The Northern European region is shaped by many different languages and small independent ethnic groups. Russia, with her large territory and millions of inhabitants, might seem an exception, however within Russia we find many different ethnic groups and cultures.

If one is to examine the characteristics of the landscapes within the Northern European region, the following picture emerges. The Atlantic spans the west, and reaches deeply into the Norwegian coastline through the mighty fjords. Fast-flowing rivers flow through Sweden down from the mountains eastwards to the Gulf of Bothnia, while Finland is shaped by its tranquil 'thousand lakes' and marshlands. The countries of Sweden, Finland, Estonia and Latvia surround the northern part of the Baltic Sea. The vast Russian landmass expands in the east, with immense slow-flowing rivers. The western part of the region lies on granite. At the west coast around the fjords and the mountains of Norway's heartland this granite rises high above the sea level. Towards the central region this granite descends into gentler formations before disappearing beneath the earth's surface. Due to the impact of powerful meteor showers, cosmic iron is present in Sweden while terrestrial iron rises up through the marshland in Finland. Towards the east we find lime, clay and areas of black earth. A long, cold and dark winter and a short powerful summer is experienced by almost all countries in the region.

Through the interaction of the forces of nature with the various landscapes a multitude of independent ethnic groups with specific languages and cultures have developed, sometimes with the gift to listen and to hear what really wants to be revealed. One also finds the tendency of holding oneself back and actively waiting. This could lead to an impression that all processes take longer with us in the north than they do elsewhere in the world. However that which arises through these processes engrains itself deeply in those people involved, and forms their lives in a natural manner.

Norway — the Camphill Village Trust

Above: Hall, Vidaråsen
Below: Theatre production, Vidaråsen

The Camphill Village Trust in Norway (**Camphill Landsbystiftelse**) was founded at Whitsun 1966, just a few months after the death of Karl König. The first effort to establish a Camphill place with many experienced Camphillers in Norway at Helgeseter near Bergen in 1954 had ground to a halt within a year. Ten years later a new call was heard from Norway, and Margit Engel inspired Phyllis and Ivan Jacobsen and Trygve Thornæs to help her answer this call. Together they purchased a small farm in the Vestfold Forest south of Oslo and moved into the old farmhouse. They did what Karl König had suggested to them: don't wait for everything to be ready, just start! Vidaråsen Landsby, the first Camphill village in Norway, was received with goodwill by the national health authorities. A new wind had started to blow and a change was due for the large institutions that helped people with special needs. After a few talks, full economic funding for the running of the village was secured. Only capital investments like building had to be raised through donations. Every year for more than fifteen years pre-university students sold beeswax candles made in the village. This candle sale made it possible to build a new house or workshop every year, and also to buy some of the properties and build up the five other Camphill places which developed over the next decade.

When Eastern Europe opened up to new impulses in the nineties, the Camphill Village Trust in Norway pioneered the development of Camphill initiatives in Estonia, Poland, Russia and Latvia, both financially and with co-workers. Thus a continuous pioneering spirit has lived in Camphill Norway.

Today the Camphill places in Norway offer life-sharing, work and cultural activities to some 140 adults with special needs. Bound together in one charitable trust, in spite of the fact that the distance between some of the places is a day's journey by car, they work closely together economically, on legal matters and on shaping our visions and goals for the 21st century.

Established in 1966, **Vidaråsen Landsby** is the oldest and biggest of the villages in Norway and is situated at Andebu in the county of Vestfold. There are currently about 120 people living in the village. The number of people with special needs is now at around fifty compared with over seventy in earlier years. This is due to a combination of an increased demand for personal space and the scarcity of applications. Besides the farm and gardens, there are various workshops such as a dairy, bakery, felting workshop, wood workshop, weavery and herb workshop. The concrete casting foundry and ceramic workshop have been very active over many years but are closed for the time being.

Fortieth anniversary celebrations, Vidaråsen

Vidaråsen Landsby has gone through many changes during the last twenty years. There has been a focusing of resources towards caring for the elderly through the building of the Ita Wegman care house in 1998. This has been a very successful project which has allowed many villagers and co-workers the chance to remain in Camphill surroundings during their last years. There has also been a marked increase in the numbers of employed staff, due to the need for more professional health workers at Ita Wegman house and because of increasing administrative duties. The positive side of this has been the gradual development of mutual openness between Vidaråsen and the surrounding community.

Hogganvik

There has been a determined effort to find new models of housing, giving a diversity of living situations that respect both co-workers and villagers' need for more privacy, offering house communities that are not based on the old extended-family model. Supporting individual development, while at the same time strengthening the community, is a challenging and ongoing task.

Vidaråsen has experimented with various organizational structures over the last years with leadership ranging from more or less flat, to attempts at clear, authoritative principles. The balance is again a challenge, to have enough structure to prevent inertia and chaos, while allowing enough openness to support group ownership and engagement.

The village community at **Hogganvik** is situated on Vinda Fjord. The village is snuggled into densely forested mountains, which rise up from the coast of the fjord. It is a small community in which 30–35 people live, with five more coming to work in the village from the surrounding neighbourhood. The community aims for a strong cultural impulse in daily life connected to the festivals. The essential areas of work are found within agriculture, the dairy, which has on a number of occasions won the best Norwegen awards for organic cheese, the garden and over 120 hectares of forest. There's also a small wood workshop and households which provide work places.

Jøssåsen was started in 1978 out of a request from parents in Sør-Trøndelag. It's a rural community which lies forty kilometres from Trondheim and seventeen kilometres from the fjord. They have a lake for swimming in summer, and mountains where they can go skiing in the winter. In the first few years they did a lot of building and expanding and today they have a farm, a weavery, a pottery and a small wood workshop. They have started a book workshop in the nearest town where they make exercise books for most of the Waldorf schools in Norway.

Above: Sheep grazing at Jøssåsen
Below: Wintertime at Jøssåsen
Bottom left: Village meeting at Jøssåsen

At present there are five house communities, 22 villagers and twenty co-workers who live at Jøssåsen, as well as six co-workers who come in everyday to work and ten villagers who come in to work part-time. These live in the local towns in small flats or house communities. Jøssåsen has a rich cultural life. Our hall houses concerts and plays and the three Camphill places in Trøndelag use it for common activities.

Solborg lies high up on a mountainside commanding sweeping views of the valley below and ridge after ridge of blue mountains. The village community was established in 1977 and consists today of about fifty people. Open to the sky it forms a magnificent setting for a farm community with a large forest, a vegetable garden and several workshops. A kindergarten and a small Waldorf school were established so co-worker children have only a few minute's walk to school. Situated in the countryside it is also near two local towns and only one hour's drive to Oslo.

Above and opposite page: images from Solborg Bottom left: Vidaråsen

Working in the gardens, Vallersund

Looking at the historical buildings in **Vallersund Gård**, one can understand how in the past this place was chosen by fishermen as a place of refuge and hospitality. Sheltered by an island from the rough Atlantic ocean and surrounded by small mountains on Norway's west coast, Vallersund Gård lies nestled in a small cove. Today six new buildings complement the old, each with their own flair, conveying a feeling of diversity and cosiness in the midst of nature's strong, impetuous forces. Vallersund Gård is a village for adults, about fifty people live here. Their experiences of the year are dominated by the calm of summer, the wind in autumn, darkness in winter and the light in spring. Everything they do in their community, whether in the school, the bakery, weavery, the herb and tea workshop, the garden, the farm or the office, is in harmony with the celebration of festivals and cultural activities. With each individual contribution, everyone with his or her own different capability, Vallersund Gård has grown over the past 28 years to be a modern place of refuge and hospitality — just like in the good old days. The Framskolen which offers a youth training programme is also situated here.

Camphill Rotvoll, the youngest branch of the Norwegian Camphill family, is already twenty years old. It's the only suburban Camphill place in Norway, just a short walk from the centre of Trondheim and situated on the Trondheim Fjord. From its tender beginnings in 1989 with just a single rented flat on a housing estate, it has expanded into a community of three houses accommodating 25–30 people. Currently there is a vegetable and herb garden, a small farm, a weavery, herb processing, a farm shop and a bakery which also delivers to Trondheim. The food processing workshop is the largest producer of biodynamic jams and juices in Norway and delivers all over the country. The farm, garden and workshops are situated on the beautiful old Rotvoll Estate, which they share with their local Waldorf school. There is work for more people than those that live here, so every week day about twenty people join them daily from the surroundings, both for work and for a common cultural life.

Above: The bakery, Vallersund
Below: Theatre production, Vallersund

Tapola, Finland

Sweden

After time spent in Camphill in Scotland, Stella Helström began curative education work in Sweden in 1965, without however being able to start a community. In 1974 a group of young villagers and co-workers moved to Delsbo in the northern part of Sweden in order to set up a much-needed Camphill village. Here forests cover hills and mountains and the two large Dellen Lakes form the backdrop for a lively and still-developing community. Starting small with a hotel and a few surrounding houses, **Camphill Staffansgården** now boasts seven units in four different neighbourhoods which can house up to 34 villagers. Three of the residential places are set aside specifically for people with mental health problems. In 1981 a farm, Mikkelsgården, was bought which up to this day bustles with a number of farm animals. A biodynamic vegetable garden supplies vegetables and potatoes. There are three residential houses within the farm neighbourhood.

In 2009 a new residential unit was bought and beautifully renovated. Four villagers live there now and a large central kitchen prepares delicious meals for the whole community. The workshops in Staffansgården, a weavery, bakery, joinery, candle workshop and the newly opened paper workshop all produce quality products and provide the villagers with meaningful work. There are sporting and cultural activities and a group of therapists including a nurse provides for the village's healthcare needs. In this way they live together through the long Swedish winters with their often deep snows and Northern Lights, and through the shorter, but magical summers with their nightly twilight.

Twenty-nine years after the first Camphill community in Sweden was founded, **Camphill Häggatorp** emerged near the small town of Vedum not far from the west coast. The community developed on a small estate with three buildings, which in the first few years required a lot of energy and time from community members for renovation work. One of these buildings serves as storage and workshop space and the other two have been developed as living spaces. It's still a small community with about twenty people. The two hectares of land are laid out like a park. The people in Häggatorp aim to integrate their workshops into the local community, especially the bakery and the biodynamic garden. In social and public realms they maintain close cooperation with their surroundings.

Finland

The Camphill Movement in Finland began through Carita Stenback in 1956 with the establishment of a small curative education home **Sylvia Koti** in Hyvinkää, southern Finland. In the mid sixties Kaarina and Freddy Heimsch came to Finland from Scotland, bringing with them years of Camphill experience. In 1970 they established the Camphill school Sylvia Koti near Lahti. Today 45 children and youths are taught and live there, and a further fifteen children take part as external pupils. In the upper classes the young people pass through a vocational training centre, in order to complete an agreed traineeship. The Sylvia building with the beautiful Swan Hall forms the cultural centre of the community. Besides celebratory functions, exhibitions, music and theatre performances there is also the possibility of a multitude of therapies.

After the first group of pupils had completed their education and training, their parents asked for living and working possibilities to be developed for their now adult sons and daughters. Maija and Aimo Kuusisto along with other co-workers

Myllylähde residents on a trip to Lappland

began to prepare for a village community for adults, and in 1974 **Tapolan Kyläyhteisö** emerged in the small village of Niinikoski, roughly thirty kilometres from Sylvia Koti.

Tapola lies in the middle of a small scattered agricultural village. Throughout the years an active and good relationship with the people of Niinikoski has developed, which is evident in mutual neighbourly help and common events, a natural form of integration. From the start the main focus of work in Tapola lay in biodynamic farming, including dairy cattle and a garden. Additionally a weavery, cheese dairy, village cafe and the households provide work places. In 2008 the village decided to build an elderly care home, to offer the elderly community members the possibility to continue living the village lifestyle after an active working life on the farm and in the workshops. Simultaneously there is an emphasis on training and work with young villagers in order to maintain the village impulse. Roughly eighty people live in Tapola Village Community and a further twenty come daily to the village to work and take part in cultural events.

The demand for residential and occupational communities in Finland continued to increase. In 1989 a group of young enthusiastic people expressed a wish to live in the sheltered surroundings of a community and in the summer of that same year **Myllylähde Community** was set up in Palomaa (Hameenkoski), a rural area

Myllylähde

approximately thirty kilometres from Lahti. Life in this village began with Aimo and Maija Kuusisto's family. There are now three households with fourteen villagers, six co-workers and four co-worker children. Here agriculture also plays a central role with both cattle and arable land being farmed. The wood workshop, weavery and craft workshop are led by two external co-workers. Cultural activities such as music (Kantele orchestra and singing), painting and eurythmy are an inherent part of the weekly activities. In 2004 the Johannessaal was built. Although a lot has changed in the community over the years, seasonal festivities celebrated together with parents and friends remain central to village life. It is through them that the people in Myllylähde receive their strength and enthusiasm, and discover the deeper meaning of community building in our times.

In recent years cooperation with the other communities in Finland has increased. This has created the possibility to discuss existing needs within our communities, and to share our enthusiasm and plans for the future. Likewise the annual meetings and common activities of the northern and eastern places have gained importance.

In 2006 the fourth Camphill community started **Kaupunkikylä** (City Village). This is a community for adults with special needs who have the wish amongst other things to be more closely connected to life in the town of Lahti. The community consists of four houses, three of which are situated within the boundaries of Sylvia-koti. The fourth and most recently acquired house is situated in a suburban area between Sylvia-koti and the city centre. It is the aim of Kaupunkikylä to create opportunities for adults with special needs to find meaningful work within the setting of the city, and to build a social network in the Lahti area where the threefold nature of society might become evident.

In Lahti town centre the community runs 'Mea Manna Eco Kahvila,' an organic café serving lunches, coffee and cakes made from biodynamic and organic ingredients. They also sell organic and biodynamic groceries. In 2010 the Kaupunkikylä bakery will begin production.

Top: Preparations for St John's festival, Tapola
Middle: Organic café, Kaupunkikylä
Bottom: Tapola

Estonia

After Estonia declared itself independent in 1991, parents of handicapped children were able to become active in looking for humane living conditions for their children. Through the Idriart cultural festivals and with the help of Margit Engel from Camphill Vidaråsen, those seeking help met with those who offered new perspectives and opportunities. Through this work, Pahkla Camphilli Küla was able to start in 1992 on a piece of land 35 kilometres south of Tallinn.

There are currently five houses, and approximately thirty people live and work in **Pahkla Camphilli Küla**, seventeen of whom are villagers. At the heart of the village is the farm, the milking cows, pastures, fields and garden. The candle workshop and weavery provide work throughout the winter months. Art and music lessons enrich life within the village. The village orchestra is also invited to give concerts outside the village. Contact with other facilities for people with special needs is maintained and many festivities, excursions and seminars take place jointly. Helping hands are always welcome during the summer with the field and garden work.

Latvia

The Camphill village in **Rozkalni** (Rosehill) is a small community in Latvia. In 1999, after spending some years in Camphill Vidaråsen, Inga and Vilnis Neimanis returned to their homeland and started to set up a Camphill community on an old farm approximately 120 kilometres north-east of Riga. Although the next sizable town, Valmiera, is only a matter of minutes away by car, Rozkalni is surrounded completely by a rural landscape. It is an agricultural community which cultivates 44 hectares of land and tends eighteen hectares of forest. They have five milking cows, goats, some sheep, chickens and a very nice donkey. Seventeen people live here and take care of the animals, the land, the forest and above all each other.

Rozkalni, Latvia

Alongside the farming, garden and estate upkeep is a lot of artistic work, with singing and above all eurythmy. The Rozkalni eurythmy group has even made some appearances on big stages. The group of villagers here changes more frequently than in other Camphill communities. This has been the case since the beginning because the young people mostly come from orphanages to Rozkalni and need help and guidance in their social lives. When, after a number of years, the young people feel strong enough to lead an independent life, they leave the community.

Russia

In 1992 Camphill was given use of a great sweep of sixty hectares of grassland lying in a bend of the river Syas, some 140 kilometres east of St Petersburg and ten kilometres south of Lake Ladoga, Europe's biggest freshwater lake. Since then four dwelling houses have been built along with a farm building, bakery and greenhouse. The building process was carried above all by co-workers such as Lars-Henrik Nesheim and Margit Engel from Camphill Vidaråsen, who came with vision, money, materials and many helping hands to create **Camphill Svetlana** from scratch.

The process of finding people to come here and make this place their home was as challenging as the building. It took some years and a lot of trial and error to build up a solid group of villagers, some of them quite limited in their abilities, and for the young and enthusiastic volunteers to become a little bit older and wiser.

Now the village is home to eighteen villagers, seven carrying co-workers, three co-worker children who attend our own village school, and seven to ten volunteers who are here for a longer or shorter periods. The farm is well established with milking cows, cheese-making, pigs, and rye, barley and oats in the fields, while the garden provides for most of the fruit and vegetable needs. Some of the people of the village have been here for ten years or more, traditions have developed, the apple trees and sea buckthorn are now bearing fruit after years of care.

The village stands as a testimony to the dedication and heroism of the many people who struggled to build it, and is today a much-respected beacon of human values to the many visitors from all levels of Russian society. Volunteers come from across Russia, and there is an increasing amount of support, also financial, which comes in the most unexpected ways. But covered in a huge blanket of snow, dealing with burst pipes, broken cars, and almost no professional help of any kind available locally, they realize that the pioneering days are not over yet!

People used to say around there that if they weren't in crisis, it wouldn't be Svetlana. The fact they manage to survive at all is a miracle, given the climate, the isolated position, the financial insecurity and last but by no means least, the heights and depths of the great Russian soul, which can fill their lives with drama, beauty, meaning, but do not promise an easy ride!

In 2001 Remco van der plaat, Olga Kourianova and Zinaida Levina founded the charitable foundation Lemniscate for the

Turmalin

furthering of curative education and social therapy, in order to have a formal body for their work. The day centre for curative education and social therapy **Turmalin** was founded by Lemniscate in 2002. It was started for young adults and youngsters and later expanded to include various groups of severely handicapped children. Today roughly thirty adults with various needs work in Turmalin and twelve children are educated there. The adults work in four workshops (pottery, candle workshop, weavery and felt-making and wood workshop). The children attend school until class ten. Almost all the co-workers have studied at university level and have an additional training in curative education and social therapy.

As it's a day centre it's particularly important to the people in Turmalin to strive to work on social threefoldness and the principles of Camphill. It is a unique and well-known organization in Moscow and receives small subsidies from the state. In the restless mega-city of Moscow, one finds in Turmalin a wonderfully peaceful atmosphere, with humour and warmth. Celebrations, plays, folk dancing and excursions into the city make life here interesting and lively.

A group of Turmalin parents who were searching for a safe place for their adult children to live approached the Lemniscate Foundation for help, and the foundation decided to start a rural village community in Russia. This idea materialized with the community **Chistye Cluchi** roughly thirty kilometres from the town of Smolensk. One residential house has already been erected and the full project is planned to accomodate sixty people including thirty villagers.

The Lemniscate Foundation has been running the Ita Wegman training course on curative education and social therapy, which is now affiliated with the Conference for Curative Education of the medical section In Dornach. This course is connected to the Moscow Pedagogical University and offers a state recognized diploma, a unique opportunity and arrangement within the Northern European region. More than one hundred people have successfully completed this seminar and more than ninety per cent of them have gone on to work in the realm of curative education in curative schools, Waldorf schools, and centres and groups for children and adults with special needs in Russia, the Ukraine, Belarus and Armenia. The training course has now opened professional training in music therapy in curative education. The majority of the teachers on the programme are from Russia and have also taught on the Baltic Seminar.

Top: Turmalin
Bottom: The first house at Chistye Cluchi

The North American region

DIEDRA HEITZMAN

The scope of Camphill in North America is large. Traversing the continent from one Camphill to another, east to west, the span is over 3,200 miles, and from north to south almost one thousand miles. An equivalent European distance would be from Lisbon to Uzbekistan, and, north to south, from Trondheim to Vienna!

Much of the work of Camphill is now receiving interest because of its particular pertinence to evolving global social and environmental challenges. The development of practical work based on anthroposophy and on the work of Karl König finds its expression in Camphill communities.

The world struggles with the care of an increasing number of people born with autism, with trying to inspire social forms that encourage dignity and self-advocacy of vulnerable citizens. They are discovering the limitations of old forms of leadership and organization and facing a huge disparity of resources, financial and otherwise, that plagues country after country. They bemoan the outcome of years of ecologically devastating agricultural practices and food distribution systems that now fail to provide necessities for much of the earth's population, while wasting tons of usable food in landfills, and they face water shortages and pollution. Can they find sustenance in spiritual forms that help in understanding the role of human beings in relation to life on earth and to the spirit?

Camphills, in their dedicated, imperfect ways, are integrating solutions and searching for realistic and practical ways to address many of these problems. This certainly is the case in North America, and while communities can easily get bogged down in internal processes and the struggle to realize ideals, still the efforts are myriad and impressive. Those efforts, while strengthening for the communities, can also be inspiring for others.

There is a diversity of expressions of Camphill, as well as an ongoing evolution. Some communities are clearly in the tradition of Camphill communities, exemplifying village life and including agriculture, as developed in the early years of the over fifty-year-old work in North America. These include Camphill

Opposite page:
Top: Triform bell choir, New York City
Middle: Strawberry pickers, Triform
Bottom: Triform

Special Schools Beaver Run, Camphill Copake, Camphill Village Kimberton Hills, Camphill Village Minnesota, Camphill Nottawasaga, Camphill Triform, Camphill Soltane, Heartbeet Lifesharing, and the Ita Wegman Fellowship.

Others have developed differently, such as the Sophia Project, which serves homeless and indigent families in a very distressed section of Oakland, California, and more urban/suburban centres such as Camphill Communities California, Camphill Sophia Creek in Ontario, The Cascadia Society in North Vancouver, British Columbia, and the Hudson Project (currently a part of Camphill Copake in New York).

In the north-east, near the Hudson River in New York State, **Camphill Copake**, the largest adult community and home to over two hundred people houses a thriving medicinal plant garden, with its concomitant healing plant products workshop and business. It is also home to Turtle Tree Seeds, a business that grows, collects and distributes biodynamic seeds nationwide, and an assortment of workshops: café, bakery, candle-making, wood workshop, weavery, book and gift shop, farm and gardens. Copake has hosted curative eurythmy training and many conferences. Because of its seniority as an adult village in the North American region, Copake was the first in the region to develop care houses for elders and has three such houses. Recognizing needs within Camphill and the local area, Copake has recently purchased a large property and is pioneering a community in Ghent, New York State, which would specialize in serving elders within an innovative co-housing village and agricultural context. Their Hudson project has placed two village households in the nearby town of Hudson, where household members volunteer in various areas of need.

Copake's neighbour, **Camphill Triform**, a youth guidance community encompassing a farm, gardens and woodlands, offers an education and student work programme. A beautiful recreational centre and bakery have recently been built. The community now includes day students, has recently become state licensed and is contemplating the purchase of nearby land for expansion.

In Pennsylvania, west of Philadelphia, is **Camphill Soltane**, the other North American youth guidance community and college. It has a programme, Soltane Works, to provide vocational training and opportunities, and in addition a community programme with semi-independent apartments for companions who have graduated and continue to live in Soltane. There is

Beaver Run

a day programme and a recently renovated orchard under the direction of a fine biodynamic orchardist.

Nearby, **Camphill Special Schools (Beaver Run)** in Glenmoore, Pennsylvania, thriving as a children's village complete with an accredited Waldorf school (K-12) for their special students, is now developing a campus for older students on the newly acquired Beaver Farm, adjacent to Kimberton Hills. The Dorian Music Therapy Training, located in Beaver Run, has graduated two classes in its four-year training programme. Beaver Run has developed college credits for its seminar in curative education, with a BA completion programme in partnership with Prescott College, a liberal arts college in Arizona. Through its seminar, it hosts a Minimum Residency Programme so that other Camphills and like-minded organizations in the region can participate. There is ongoing work towards a programme that might result in Camphill being able to grant degrees, although that is in the research stage at the time of this writing. In addition, Beaver Run seminar teachers have taught curative education workshops in Mexico, Kyrgyzstan, Thailand, Russia and Taiwan. Following Beaver Run's example, Camphill Copake can also grant college credits for its seminar in social therapy.

Kimberton

Camphill Village Kimberton Hills, in Kimberton Pennsylvania, always with a significant emphasis on biodynamic land work, also has an ongoing presence in the world of sustainable living and design. With the presence of Camphill Architect's Joan Allen, the community's buildings and ecological practices have created many tours as an ecovillage. The community has won awards for its agriculture, sustainability and cultural venue, and serves the surrounding community through its Community Supported Agriculture gardens (CSA), dairy, bakery and café, as well as musical and other cultural events. One of the more publically accessible communities, it is nevertheless one of the larger in terms of land with 432 acres (173 hectares). It has created successful partnerships with local businesses, some of which are hosted on the property. Kimberton Hills remains unlicensed and generates one quarter of its income through its own activities.

Through the presence of the Camphill communities and Waldorf schools in New York and Pennsylvania, the surrounding regions have seen growth in various areas: organic and biodynamic food production and distribution, training opportunities involving anthroposophy, sustainable business practices, interest in mission-related investing, anthroposophical medical practices and therapies, the arts and the work of the Christian Community.

Kimberton

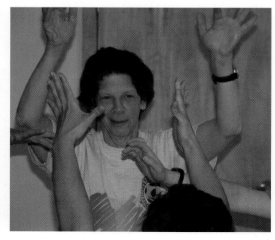

The northernmost community, **Heartbeet** in Hardwick, Vermont is a young and thriving community, the newest Camphill, with three households and a biodynamic farm. Two of its three founders were born and spent their childhood in Kimberton Hills, and the third was a co-worker there. Heartbeet has a special emphasis on partnerships and innovative social integration with businesses and services in their area. It has created and hosts twice yearly intensive and successfully growing conferences for young people interested in anthroposophy.

Moving toward the Toronto region of Canada, **Camphill Nottawasaga**, sister community of the more urban Sophia Creek, together known as Camphill Ontario, has re-established its community structure and is the only Camphill in North America that has a non-resident Executive Director, a condition of its province's funding. It has some non-resident house managers. It has a strong emphasis on care of the land and handicrafts. **Sophia Creek** consists of three houses, other associated neighborhood buildings and workshops in a residential neighborhood of Barrie. In its efforts to be a part of the surrounding community, it has increasingly exemplified community building and culture, including crafts workshops. One of the houses is owned by a person with disabilities, and they are active in the Novalis Project, which brings cultural events to the Novalis Hall, located in Nottawasaga.

California

Camphill Village Minnesota is a land-based community of 470 acres (188 hectares), a two-hour drive north-west of Minneapolis, on the rolling central plains of Minnesota, with woodlands tucked into the valleys and along its pastures. Their recently built village centre and hall includes a processing kitchen serving food processing needs of neighbouring farms, as well as its own garden. The village's other crafts include a bakery, weaver, woodworking shop, card shop and hemp jewellery shop. The extremes of weather are invigorating and create a strong emphasis on home and healthy village cultural life. Its connections with the surrounding farm and small town neighbours are strong.

To the south of St Louis is a Camphill affiliate, **Oakwoods Lifesharing** in West Plains, Missouri. Its two households are integrated in their rural neighbourhood, with much neighbourly and civic support. Sheltered by many Ozark-type Oaks, the community has weathered challenges by governmental agencies and has become a model of care for people with disabilities in the state. The need for good and dignified care for people with disabilities in this area has been recognized as significant, as the state has witnessed serious instances of abuse and neglect in support agencies in recent years.

California

Within sight of the Pacific Ocean near the west coast of the United States in Soquel, California, is **Camphill Communities California**, comprising five homes; organic vegetable, flower and herb gardens; a small vineyard and orchard; and a weaving workshop. Artistic and cultural pursuits and festival celebrations are central to daily life. The community partners with local service organizations to enrich the cultural, artistic and social lives of people with disabilities in the wider Santa Cruz community. The community affiliates with the **Sophia Project** in Oaklands, California, as it strives to address the needs of homeless and disadvantaged families.

Northward to beautiful Canadian British Columbia are two distinct Camphill communities. **The Cascadia Society** is integrated into a North Vancouver neighbourhood and houses a cultural/therapeutic and educational centre for those adults who live in their four neighborhood homes and others who join for day activities. **The Ita Wegman Association — Glenora Farm** is a growing and evolving agriculturally based community on Vancouver Island. Their recent work in sustainable buildings is admirable, and they are able to harvest not only vegetables, but also windfall wood they mill for their buildings and other uses.

The Camphill Association of North America has encouraged and supported communities in finding ways to develop themselves in alignment with the ideals of Camphill and with the changing conditions of our time. That has meant encouraging learning circles, conferences, events and outreach as well as association in the areas of education, sustainability, co-worker development and expansion. Clear guidelines for association membership and affiliations have been helpful, as well as focusing on the need for increased recognition of the spiritual basis of Camphill to guide decision making. The Camphill Association has also aligned itself with The North American Council for Curative Education and Social Therapy, and with its connection to the medical section of the Anthroposophical Society. This council has members beyond Camphill who are also working out of anthroposophy and often in the life-sharing models similar to Camphill.

From east to west, north to south, Camphill is alive and thriving on the North American continent. Its work is constantly evolving to meet challenges and needs and is well suited for these times.

The Southern African region

South Africa

JULIAN SLEIGH

The final decade of the last century saw a remarkable political and social change in the state of South Africa. The era of apartheid was brought to an end and a radical process of transformation began. It was undoubtedly miraculous the way an imposed and restrictive regime made way for the various races, social groups and diverging cultural and economic interests to open the floodgates of change. A new and inspired constitution united the various factions and fostered the spirit of reconciliation and consensus. This supported the existing welfare institutions and meant that privilege ceased to be the bonus of a particular racial group.

This positive approach had three main effects on the work of Camphill in the country. First and foremost our centres became open to all racial groups. This brought together the privileged and the distinctly under-privileged, outright poor and at risk residents that filled the waiting lists and the vacancies as they arose. Diverging habits of living, eating, language, values, entertainment and the handling of money and resources all called for positive acceptance and adjustment.

The second main effect of 'transformation' has been a decline in the number of Camphill-trained carrying co-workers coming from Europe. This is in part due to a government policy of affirmative action that restricts the granting of work permits to foreign would-be immigrants. It means that the mature Camphill way of life has had to be modified, one could say compromised. Space has therefore been made for administrators, house leaders, work-masters, carers and helpers coming from quite varied cultures. A healthy challenge to our aim of community building!

A third aspect of adjustment has been to modify our way of renumerating co-workers. Individual wages and salaries have become a more frequent feature of the working arrangements. The time-honoured working for no regular payment remains an option.

The management of one of our centres found that the reliance on 'destiny' to produce the team of necessary co-workers was too

Girls in the vegetable garden, Botswana

precarious. It decided to sever its connection to the Camphill Movement in 2006. This was the **Cresset House Village** in the northern area of Johannesburg. The parting of ways was amicable and some contact remains.

Thus Camphill has three remaining centres in South Africa, all in the Western Cape reasonably near to Cape Town. There is the Camphill school near the seaside town of **Hermanus** that offers residential curative education and therapy to children with special needs, which extends into youth guidance for those in adolescence.

Adjacent to the school is the **Camphill Farm Community** for adults: a village with a farm, gardens, workshops and nine group homes. The two centres share the Phila Therapy Centre and the magnificent Mercury Hall.

Fifty kilometres north of Cape Town is the **Camphill Village West Coast**. This has twelve house communities, large and small, and an extensive organic and biodynamic farm, orchards, plant and tree nursery, gardens, a dairy, bakery and herbal workshop, a chapel, community centre, the Moya Health and Therapy Centre, a food processing workshop and a café. There is also a comprehensive department for building maintenance.

Suppertime in Botswana

Botswana

R ICHARD B LAKE

Community life in Botswana finds expression in particular ways: a strong culture of singing together and closeness to prayer, an honouring of tradition, including the respect for old age and those who have gone before. There is also a tolerance to each other born out of close living to the land, in a country where the rain sometimes does not come. All are expressed both in ceremony and in daily life. At the same time much is changing with the assimilation of global culture and the rapid development of infrastructure. This is a source of pride, satisfaction and confidence among people. These diverse aspects of rapid change and a respect for tradition often live side by side.

Community life in the Camphill communities in Botswana is no exception. From a modest beginning in 1974, with many small steps, three Camphill communities — school, training centre and village — have grown on a twelve hectare site on the edge of a large village called **Otse**. The village is surrounded by hills and is situated in the south-east corner of Botswana. Over

Above: Kindergarten
Below: The football team

two hundred people are part of the communities. People who have joined or spent time, either as pupils, trainees, employees or volunteers, have often had opportunities to unfold through the experience of learning, meeting, supporting each other and through facing the challenges of personal and community development. This opportunity to unfold is at the heart of Camphill communities' work. The Bible Evening, services and celebration of the festivals are also valued and upheld.

The Camphill communities continue to build links with wider society. By interacting closely with the Ministry of Education and Botswana Training Authority, work continues to ensure that what Camphill offers is part of mainstream provision and is adaptive to national priorities. Grassroots activity continues, working with local disability support groups in four local villages, supporting initiatives to develop services, particularly around issues of HIV/Aids. Networking with the wider Camphill Movement continues through the Camphill Africa Regional Association and further afield, building links between the Association of Camphill Communities in the UK and Ireland and the Camphill Africa region.

Light in Botswana — the clear glancing rays of dawn, the midday shimmering glare, the setting evening glow and then the luminous expanse of stars — all give a very different experience than the image of the candle shining out through the cold northern night, and yet our three Camphill communities here in Botswana feel deeply connected with the wider Camphill impulse.

Pupils at Legodimo

Camphill outreach into other cultures

Introduction

Richard Steel

Whereas it's relatively straightforward to investigate and assess the history and development of the Camphill Movement, it becomes more and more questionable how to define the movement at present and how to discern if an initiative or even an established institution can conform to the criteria of the movement. Perhaps this is understandable in an age when individualism is in the fore and is necessary for the diverse settings and tasks that need to be addressed and can be embraced by such a movement attempting a truly holistic approach.

Surely wherever centralism, normalization and streamlining in whatever guise reveals itself, the contemporary mind, heart and will are called upon to ensure the existence and significance of minorities, of diversity and here-and-now solutions. The Camphill Movement never had in that sense a catalogue of criteria, nor a formalized membership procedure to hinder spontaneous developments and ongoing dialogue process. In this sense the question is not new, but one never ceases to be amazed how future-bearing König's way of proceeding was. He distinguished from the beginning between the concepts 'Camphill' and 'Camphill Movement,' even describing them as two different entities — as mother and child. Often today the differentiation is made between 'Camphill community', referring to those connecting to each other in their inner striving towards the ideals and impulses intended by König, and 'Camphill Movement,' referring to the outer expression of this work — the institutions in a wider sense, formed out of and consciously relating to the Camphill impulse. And always the question must be kept alive of the delicate but existential relationship between a community carrying inner convictions and striving for realization on the one hand and outer manifestations on the other; compromise and alignment with outer circumstances being both a precondition for effectiveness and pitfall at the same time.

König ended his annual report of the Camphill Movement 1960 with the following words:

> I cannot conclude without asking a fundamental
> question which we have also asked ourselves in the
> Council of the Movement when we met a fortnight
> ago: What is the connection between Camphill itself
> and the Camphill Movement? ... Is it perhaps so,
> that Camphill has to sacrifice itself in order that
> the Movement may grow? Or is it rather so that the
> Movement will work back on to Camphill in order to
> rejuvenate it? I would not dare to give an answer, but
> I would beg you, dear friends, to keep this question
> in mind, to move it in your hearts, because it is a very
> important question. And again only life will teach
> us to give the right answer ... Now we have to be
> very watchful, very careful, to see what the mother,
> Camphill, is expecting from the Movement — what
> the child needs of the mother; and how these two
> entities are going to work together ... The Movement
> asks a great deal of Camphill; and whether Camphill
> will be able to answer, and in which way it will be
> able to answer, is to be seen.
> (Karl König, *Report of the Camphill Movement*,
> January 28,1960. Unpublished manuscript, Karl
> König Archive)

Certainly König never saw the impulse that he connected with the name 'Camphill' to be tied down or limited to a specific style of institution — or even to a specific task for that matter. The essay he wrote at the end of his life, after the rich experience in community building for the curative setting, is quite an opening towards the future:

> A so-called welfare society which starts to forget
> human values — a human race which denies racial
> problems and has invented at the same time means
> of mass destruction that can kill millions in a few
> minutes — a social order which forgot the divine
> order and searches for new ethics that can't be
> found any more because of the loss of belief in
> God — this generates a new array of tasks: to help

the frail, disabled, lame and sick persons, and those
who have become defenceless and depressive to
gain once more their human dignity. Is it not a great
miracle? Mankind on the brink of self-destruction
creates something new that grows like a new seed
within a sinking society. A holistic curative education
resembles the developing seed in a rotting fruit. We
only need to define the concept of curative education
widely enough, to see its true purpose ... it's intention
is to become a global task that can help counteract
the 'threat to the individual person' which has arisen
everywhere. The 'curative-educational approach'
needs to express itself in every field of social
work, in pastoral care, in the care for the elderly,
in the rehabilitation of mentally ill and physically
handicapped people, in the guidance of orphans and
refugees, of suicide candidates and the desperate; but
also in development aid, in the international Peace
Corps and similar ambitions. This is the only answer
we have today — in as much as we still want to be
human beings — for a society dancing on the brink of
disaster.
('The Purpose and Value of Curative-Educational
Work', *The Child with Special Needs*)

It seems to speak for itself that König was not only thinking
of the communities as they had been up to that point, but
hoped that the experience gained in them could ray out into
society wherever it was needed. This definitely speaks to the
individualistic approach of our times, and finds echoes in the
work of many individuals and groups working in such diverse
situations, for instance, as social work in Aboriginal settlements
in Australia; working with street children in the slums of big
cities; with abused children and their mothers; with youngsters
after substance abuse; keeping contact with those imprisoned,
and finding new ways of helping the elderly. 'Camphill' reaches
out beyond the communities creating a new sense of 'Movement.'
    In his Camphill Movement Report of 1959 Karl König had
already been clear about the necessity to widen out:

Is the Movement identical with curative education
only? It is not. Where the image of man is distorted
and humiliated, the Movement has its place.

And one year later he was happy to be able to report about 'the tree of Camphill' already showing two new buds — the care for the land and the penetration of design and architecture with spiritual intentions, which had begun to form themselves as tasks in their own rights. In 1960, he added:

> Today we are able to say: where the image of
> man and the earth is distorted and humiliated, the
> Movement is going to have its place.
> (*Reports of the Camphill Movement*, 1959 and 1960.
> Unpublished manuscripts, Karl König Archive)

Camphill as an inner impulse for healing and furthering the human being, social life and the earth out of insights to be found in the new spiritual science Rudolf Steiner had inaugurated: this had begun of course at a specific time and within the wider geographic area of Europe and with specific needs of children. This must certainly be seen as a special destiny and — as König called it on various occasions — as 'a miracle that wants to reveal itself.' Nevertheless from this pioneer situation he hoped more would evolve. Thus he concluded his report, looking forwards:

> And this is another important step, because we have
> now to work for curative education — and this will
> continue; and with this perhaps all our new settlements
> may start. But we have now also the branch of the
> Village; and, dear friends, it will not always be a village
> for handicapped young men and women — it may
> be, in all that is going to come, that it will be a village
> for stranded people, a village in Africa for black and
> coloured people, a village in Malaya, a village here and
> there; because the economic life of the world is going to
> break down, and village seeds will have to be sown here
> and there and in many other places. Therefore I foresee
> this branch as a most important one — not confined
> at all to Botton and the Grange, but giving many more
> possibilities if we are permitted and allowed to start
> them.
>
> Intimately connected with this is the new bud. It
> is not more than a bud, but a bud which will grow
> into the care for the land, for which should grow and
> ripen, for the soil, for the earth altogether. Perhaps

more branches are going to come, but also this is part of self-recognition for the Movement, because now it begins to sprout into several directions.

In this respect, it is surely fitting to close this section about the regions of the Camphill Movement with descriptions of initiatives for community building growing out of Camphill, but with open questions as to region and 'Movement' in the old sense and as to the true meaning of new cosmopolitan Christianity — something that was deep in the heart of Karl König.

Sadhana Village

Vasant Deshpande

Sadhana Village is a community of around thirty adults with special needs living in four houses at the heart of the Kolwan Valley in Pune district, India. There are housemothers, co-workers and volunteers sharing their life together.

Our connection with Camphill goes back to the late eighties. We wanted to start a residential care centre for adults with developmental disabilities but our experience with other centres in India had left us utterly disappointed. We therefore placed an enquiry in an international forum asking for information about the care and rehabilitation of mentally challenged adults. The only response we got was from Copake Camphill Village, from a fellow Indian, Kumar Mal.

Information about the Camphill Movement began to flow in. A group of co-workers from Copake visited us in India, and members of our core group were sponsored in 1990 to visit Copake and study the movement in action. This cooperation has continued to this day. How did the exposure to Camphill Copake affect us?

The rural setting, the practice of extended family life, and the concept of dealing not with a disabled person but with an individual who happens to be disabled are so tantalizingly Indian. Added to this we came to find that the Camphill Movement is imbued with a spiritual content which incorporated the age-old Eastern concepts of karma and reincarnation. No wonder we felt so eager to create a Camphill type village in India.

Establishing a new village calls for effort, ingenuity and a lot of humility. Things work only when destiny is strongly and

The drum circle

persistently on your side. We bought a small plot of land in a valley with a meandering river. We constructed four rooms and Medha and Rajni moved in. We then consulted friends who were working in the disability sector about available resources. Almost all of them were accessing government grants for their projects. They advised us not to go to the government for grants if we wanted to do something original. They also told us how hard it is to attract talented workers to stay and work in the countryside.

Meanwhile in 1995 a few friends associated with Camphill initiated a day-care centre for special persons in Bangalore. After some months they decided to close it down and asked us if we could accommodate two or three of their special friends.

After the first flush of starting the village, we sat down to comprehensively review our situation. The first thing was to decide on whether we wanted to copy a western model in all its details; the second was about our existing spiritual moorings, and the third was about the financial resources.

Our decision was to set up a thoroughly Indian village, already at the back of our mind when we had earlier decided on the name Sadhana: a hallowed concept from the Hindu and the Buddhist philosophies. The word 'village' was to affirm our family relationship with the Camphill Movement.

We decided to adhere to the basic Camphill concept of keeping the person with special needs at the centre of our work. We call such a person a 'special friend.' We share our lives, respecting his/her dignity, accepting without reservation that she/he could be our teacher in many things and offering unstinted love.

We also decided to follow the Camphill routine of daily life. The day in Sadhana begins and ends with prayers. There is the equivalent of the weekly Bible Evening. We celebrate Indian festivals like Diwali and Ganesh Chaturthi. Since we always have some Christian volunteers, we also celebrate Christmas and Easter with great enthusiasm.

Like in Copake, the core group of co-workers are not paid salaries for their work; we have, however, other salaried employees working for our village.

We decided to participate in the life of the rural communities around us. We assist some families to set up irrigation schemes, we help women victims of domestic violence to stand up and fight for their rights, and we have been running educational projects. Recently we started a school for children on Waldorf lines. We

The king and his vizier!

in Sadhana, including the special friends, have benefited more from these activities than the rural families around us. Our special friends are invited to weddings and community feasts. Our co-workers and housemothers are less stressed out as they find relief and rejuvenation while working with the rural families around.

As Indians we have a strong tradition of spirituality in our life. The Upanishads speak of universality and a total absence of dogmatism. By subscribing to karma and reincarnation, anthroposophy has revived in modern times a fresh Upanishadic quest for esoteric integrity and universality. There is a great need to explore the higher worlds thrown open by Rudolf Steiner. Not for nothing has he called anthroposophy a spiritual science. Science needs an open mind, a dedicated spirit of enquiry and humility to recognize that there are different ways of encountering the ocean, the Paramatman.

Sadhana Village has few sources of income. The parents of special friends contribute to the village to some extent. We have been helped by friends from abroad, including the East West Fund USA, to meet some of our capital needs. We still have a yawning deficit every year. We try to rely more and more on local resources, but in the absence of government and other institutional support it's a long haul.

The Lord says in the Bhagawadgita: remember Me, and fight on!

'Yes, I've got a point to make!'

Friends of Camphill India

FRANCIS ARADHYA AND URSULA CHOWDHURY

Friends of Camphill India is a residential community located at the outskirts of the city of Bangalore in South India. After a humble beginning as a day centre in a private apartment, we opened the doors of the first new house in 1999 and planted the first coconut, mango and papaya trees. The trees have been growing slowly and steadily and so have we.

In the community we have two big family houses, Antaranga and Santvana, which are home to 24 men and women with mental disabilities, nine co-workers' children, nine permanent Indian co-workers and about six volunteers from abroad. The third building Panchanga is home to four different workshops, and harbours a beautiful space for celebrations, cultural activities, games and yoga. For the last nine months we also have a cowshed with mother and calf. The houses are surrounded by gardens where we grow organic vegetables and fruits, keeping the many monkeys at bay. Biodynamic compost-making started last year.

In terms of our working life we hardly differ from other Camphill communities. We put a great deal of emphasis on the importance and value of the contributions of each and every individual in the community. The belief that work is worship has never been lost in India. We thrive well through a fresh recognition of this valuable attitude.

True to another aspect of the Indian cultural and spiritual life, we have developed a very rich and colourful chain of festivals throughout the year. It's a great joy for all that we celebrate both Hindu and Christian festivals with equal enthusiasm, fervour, creativity and respect.

Every Saturday evening we step out of our daily routine and come together for an Antaranga evening. 'Antaranga' is the Kannada word for 'the inner part of our heart.' It is a word that refers to a space in our deeper soul regions, delicate, subtle and yet strong by its very nature. It is a sphere beyond religion, beyond our human differences. With silence, poetry, devotional songs, short stories and even more silence we try to be together at that moment, approaching that space.

As a community we also try to support the further growth of anthroposophical curative education and social therapy in South India. With this as our aim we are conducting three-year part-time foundation courses with the help of experienced Camphill co-workers from America, Scotland, Ireland, Holland and other countries. The first course was completed in 2007. The second course started in the fall of 2009. These courses have already benefited about thirty students. Several members of the teaching faculty have expressed their great joy at the overwhelming eagerness and openness in the students' attitudes. We can honestly say that it is our whole community that makes it possible to conduct these courses. The students stay in the community for two weeks twice a year. These weeks are indeed intense and filled with extra house chores, cultural events and human encounters.

Our community is built on the land of an ashram in the vicinity of a Ganesha temple. The land is not large enough to expand in a big way. However, we feel the need for one more building, as we get many visitors and our seminar participants need accommodation, but most importantly, some of our elder residents need a quieter place in a smaller household. We have started conversations with our architect and we anticipate starting the construction of one more house as soon as possible. With this house we will come to the completion of our intention to create a residential community for about sixty people.

Community living comes naturally to most Indians. The concept of a joint family structure is very familiar and the capacity to adjust, to share and to care flows easily out of the Indian soul. The impulse of living in a community together with people who have special needs is, however, quite new to India. The great challenge we co-workers have in Friends of Camphill India is to see that all of us grow more towards becoming responsible and equal individuals who perform out of our own free will. There is a long way to go but we can truly say that the anthroposophical impulse is incarnating into the ancient Spirit of the East.

Friends of Camphill India

A Camphill inspired initiative in Vietnam

HA VINH THO

The Vietnam War ended in 1975. It had lasted over thirty years and left the country badly destroyed, with most of the infrastructures bombed, and some three to four million Vietnamese from both sides killed.

Early in the American military effort it was decided that since the enemy were hiding their activities under triple-canopy jungle, a useful first step might be to defoliate certain areas. The defoliants were distributed in drums marked with colour-coded bands, most famously Agent Orange which contained dioxin. About twelve million gallons (45,000,000 litres) of Agent Orange were sprayed over South-east Asia during the American involvement.

The Vietnamese government estimates that there are over four million victims of dioxin poisoning in Vietnam. These chemicals continue to change the landscape, cause diseases and birth defects, and poison the food chain. Although there are no independent scientific research statistics available, it seems reasonable to assume that the high proportion of children with birth defects and other disabilities was, and still is, related to this problem.

After the end of the war in 1982, I had the opportunity to go back to Vietnam. I had been working and living in a Camphill community (Perceval Switzerland) with my wife Lisi and our two children since 1977. At the time the country was barely recovering from the consequences of the war and the situation of the children living with disabilities and their families was very difficult. There were hardly enough schools for regular primary education, and special education was not a high priority.

Lisi and I created the Eurasia Association, which later became a foundation, in an attempt to solve this difficult situation. The objectives were to foster the development and social integration of mentally and physically disabled individuals and children living in Vietnam; and to strive for recognition of, and respect for, their dignity and rights.

What began as a modest financial support for children and their families gradually evolved into training teachers in curative education and creating special schools. Later, we invited seven Vietnamese students to attend full training in Camphill Perceval.

All of them are now back in Vietnam, and four of them work directly with the Eurasia Foundation.

To this day, the Eurasia Foundation has created seven special schools with various local partners, as well as several vocational training workshops. Over three hundred children have passed through our schools.

Until recently, we felt the situation was not ripe to create a life and work community that would be directly inspired by the Camphill model. Two years ago, the situation changed. We realized how difficult it for the youngsters from our schools to find vocational training and a place to live once they finish primary education. It was our Vietnamese co-workers who expressed their will to create a community based on the same values and principles they had experienced when training and visiting in various Camphill places. Out of the needs of the youngsters, the wish of the parents and the will of our Vietnamese co-workers, the Peaceful Bamboo Family was born.

About twenty friends from Camphill, Switzerland, came to Vietnam for the opening ceremony on Easter Sunday in April 2009, in Hue. We organized an evening with all these friends and our staff to share 'what is Camphill' on the night before the opening. It appeared to us that at the heart of this question is 'true human encounter' — with our children and villagers, but also between all of us.

Today, the Peaceful Bamboo Family is a striving community with twenty residents and three day students. We have well-functioning workshops making traditional paintings on wood, fruit preserves, ice cream and embroidery. There is also an organic garden and guest rooms. We have a committed team of well-trained co-workers and many projects for the future, including a training centre in partnership with the University of Hue.

Not being affiliated to the government or to a religious institution, the Peaceful Bamboo Family needs friends, it needs to feel 'part of a community.' There is a genuine will from the side of our Vietnamese co-workers to be part of the Camphill Movement and to belong to something bigger than their daily work in Hue.

Many questions are still open: how can Camphill manifest in a totally different surrounding? How can Vietnamese culture, spirituality, history, social, economic and political context be taken into account, without diluting the fundamental values and principles of Camphill?

These questions and challenges are an opportunity to explore different ways to manifest Camphill in our time.

The Camphill impulse in Romania

JOHN BYRDE

When the Iron Curtain fell in 1989, several occasions arose to present the possibilities of anthroposophical curative education and social therapy in Eastern Europe, and many people from east and west responded. A window of opportunity had opened and a flurry of initiatives began. That window began to close all too soon, from 1993, as attention turned to Iraq and later the Balkan wars.

What could Camphill offer these countries that had become 'cultural deserts' in which people with disabilities had been kept out of sight and out of mind, as poor reflections of the Communist tenet that 'man is a product of society?' It took us some time to realize that the enthusiasm for the life shown in the Camphill films of Jonathan Stedall was for the material well-being rather than the community impulse. In fact 'community' was a dirty word and anything 'commun-' evoked visceral reactions. Nevertheless, what could be shared was true respect for the other, the quest for a true image of man, a worldview that allowed man's spiritual dimension to find expression, and a striving in which a deep-rooted orthodox piety could thrive.

The Camphill impulse indeed had much to offer in post-1989 Romania, but the Camphill way of life appealed to very few for their own biographies. In any case, the authorities in Romania — and remember, if governments had been changed by events, administrations had been little affected — made it clear that while curative education was welcome and much needed, independent centres were unthinkable unless financed entirely from outside.

So it was in that context that curative education and later social therapy centres became established. At Simeria and Urlati, the ministry concerned opened new state centres in partnership with the newly founded associations set up by the Romanian initiative groups with their European friends. At Simeria the school catered for the whole district and a network of support services has developed for children and their families as well as a social therapy centre. At Urlati the focus was on the de-institutionalization and education of children abandoned to state care. By 1996 the associations had set up an official curative education training course — of course, in partnership with the state.

For ten to twelve years the centres thrived, with considerable professional, financial and material support from centres abroad across the whole spectrum of the curative movement, not only Camphill. Good personal relations with key people in the national and county administrations were of fundamental importance and helped us through several critical periods when other powers-that-be were less enchanted with these cosmopolitan initiatives, dancing to other tunes.

With Romania's imminent accession to the European Union, hopes were revived to move beyond existing institutional and administrative constraints. But the sweeping EU-inspired reforms brought only more bureaucracy, higher standards to meet with, less resources, and increasing interference by county officials who had inherited the decentralized powers of national authorities but not their wider perspective. Thus the declared rights of people with disabilities and the legislative framework may be compared with those in Western Europe, but social attitudes lagged fifty years behind. Administration in particular was overly governed by nepotism, corruption and self-interest, and obsessed with control and manipulation of the social process.

Yet our centres (including two other initiatives in Bucharest) have a high profile and are appreciated by state and public alike for the quality of their work and the initiatives they take.

Romania has (re)entered Europe, but a Europe that has still to find an identity that initiative-bearers can relate to, and that holds in check prevailing national tendencies which have little concern for with those marginalized and excluded from society. The problems get deeper, the challenges greater.

Where are the springs that can nourish such oases?

The words Karl König wrote in the last months of his life speak ever clearer today:

> Only support from person to person,
> the encounter of a self with another self —
> the awareness of the other person's individuality —
> without questioning the other's religion,
> convictions or political background,
> but simply the gaze from eye to eye, between two
> personalities —
> only this creates the kind of curative education
> which can, in a healing way, counteract the threat
> to our innermost humanity.
> ('The Purpose and Value of Curative-Educational
> Work', *The Child with Special Needs*)

6. Community — the Social Form of the Future

ANDREW PLANT

For seventy years Camphill has had a successful history of developing inclusive communities whose central task is based upon creating a home, education, training, work, care and support for people with disabilities. A task of equal significance revolves around community itself — creating, sustaining and developing community out of the conviction that community is the social form of the future and has enormous potential for both personal transformation and for social renewal.

Underpinning and inspiring the daily work of the Camphill communities worldwide is the belief — arising from Rudolf Steiner's anthroposophy — that the evolution of humanity unfolds through successive stages of development. The human race began in a time of what could be called group consciousness and then developed to our time of individualization and ego consciousness. Steiner, along with many other visionary writers and philosophers, saw that the future will be a time of universality and of global unity.

We can begin to prepare for this next step of human development through creating community today. Through living and working together in communities that promote harmony and mutual support; that serve the spiritual development of each person; that strive to bring healing to individuals, to society and to the earth, we actively engage in making manifest the potential of the future.

Throughout history some people, motivated by a reaction to religious, economic, political or social changes, have removed themselves from mainstream society and established communities as places in which they could live out their ideals in peace. The motivation of the people who founded and joined these communities has not just been to distance themselves from the perceived evils of mainstream society. They have also been moved by the conviction that they have been called to create a better society, a heaven on earth.

However, it is no easy task to create and sustain such alternative social realities. A great amount of energy and vision is needed to hold people together and these communal enterprises are both marginal and vulnerable. Most intentional communities collapse within the first few years; few surviving beyond the death of their founder and those that do manage to survive longer are not immune from pressures from their host society and from internal difficulties. The longer communities survive, the more they change and develop. Over time, most communities become less radical, less idealistic and less marginal. Ironically, just those factors that promote community stability and success, such as a larger and more diverse membership, more resources and more efficient organization, also serve to take the edge off and even undermine collective values.

We can trace a similar path in the development of the Camphill communities. Although my immediate experience is limited to Camphill in Great Britain and Ireland, what I have read and heard leads me to believe that — despite the differences in circumstances from one region to another, and despite the obvious differences in size and age — some general principles of community development hold good. These principles indicate that intentional communities move through recognizable and archetypal phases of development. This is not to say that the progress through these phases is predetermined. It is rather the case that an appreciation of the general evolution of communities provides insights that can be of use in developing the appropriate social forms, organizational structures, attitudes and outlooks that are in tune with the phase that the community is going through. In this way we are better able to engage with the change occurring in the communities in a proactive and positive manner.

In the pioneering phase Camphill was founded on the charismatic and visionary leadership of Dr Konig. The first communities were intense and idealistic, their members inspired by the insights of anthroposophy and the leadership and guidance of Dr Konig. The early pioneers and founders of Camphill devoted themselves wholeheartedly to the life and work, the responsibility and the tasks involved in creating and developing the communities. Each person willingly conformed to the expectations of communal life, and put the needs of the community before their own interests. There was little in the way of money and resources but a great amount of energy and enthusiasm. There was a very strong sense of being called to take part in a unique personal, social, cultural and spiritual task. There was also a strong sense of identity — an identity that was very separate from the world 'outside.'

As time progressed and the communities have increased in size and in numbers, in diversity and complexity, other aspects have begun to come to the fore. It is still the case that in many communities there are strong personalities in leadership positions, but in addition, responsibility has been shared out to mandated groups. Many aspects of community life have been reviewed and rationalized and have became better organized. Partly out of a need to run communities more efficiently and partly as a response to external intervention and requirements, new management principles are now firmly in place.

This next phase of development has been characterised — in the communities in Britain at least — by policies and procedures, care standards, inspections, new management structures, training and qualifications and governance. Also in recent years there has been an expansion in the number of both offices and carparks. There are more offices to deal with the increase in management and administration and there are more car parks in order to cope with the number of people attending and visiting the communities on a daily basis. There has been an overall decline in the number of co-workers and residents living in the communities and an increase in the number of day attenders and employees.

A large number of people have been employed, not only to replace unsalaried and residential co-workers but also to fill the new posts that have been required to run the communities — often posts that require specialist skills and expertise.

At the same time the communities have also witnessed a process of increasing individualization. On the one hand the co-workers have begun to articulate their needs for more balance in their lives between the competing demands of community, work and personal and family time. On the other hand there has been a growing recognition within the communities that communities can only prosper through encouraging each person — each pupil, resident, co-worker and employee — to develop to their full potential. As a result there has been a new mood of empowerment and inclusion.

Parallel to all of these processes, many of the communities in Britain have also experienced something of a decline in the vitality of the cultural and spiritual activities that had previously been defining features of Camphill life. The implications of a more diverse and tolerant community ethos and the rise of individualization and individual freedom and choice seem to be that there is less interest in taking part in the traditional community celebrations and other communal events.

Over the last years, the communities in Britain have had to face a succession of major challenges both internal and external. There has been the need to integrate and comply with the ongoing series of new regulations to do with education and care provision; the need to adapt to new systems of management and governance, and there have been issues of over-funding and questions over the 'strategic relevance' of community as a setting for care and support for people with learning disabilities. In addition, internal conflict on various levels has continued to be a factor of community life, which has marred the experience of community and led to critical situations in some Camphill centres. At a time when many residential co-workers are becoming older and wishing to hand over their responsibilities, there are also concerns over how to find new people to live in the communities and carry them forward, and how to uphold Camphill ideals and practices in a time of an increasingly diverse workforce.

The responses to these challenges have varied from person to person, from community to community and from issue to issue. There has been a certain degree of wariness and resistance but there has also been positive engagement and optimism.

The signs are that some of the communities are in state of transition from previous phases of development to yet another new phase — a phase that is going to require new answers to the challenges inherent in times of increasing diversity and complexity. In these transitional situations, it seems that the traditional ways of doing things are no longer as effective or as vital as they used to be and yet the new ways of doing things have not yet fully emerged.

This can be a time of uncertainty, and yet in this uncertainty there can also be a sense of confidence that is grounded on all that Camphill has so far achieved over the seventy years of its development. There is much to celebrate over these last years. Camphill communities have powerfully influenced the lives of many people. They have shown that it's possible to create a shared lifestyle based on mutual support, economic cooperation, communal celebration and a belief in the active influence of the spiritual world in the life of each individual and in the community as a whole. The Camphill communities have only managed to achieve so much through being prepared to go through a continual process of adaptation and through responding to changing circumstances and changing needs. The potential for the future development of the communities lies in an inner sense of confidence, coherence and resilience that has been developed over the years.

It seems that in Britain, the time of pioneering and establishing new communities is over. It's now a time of coming to terms with and integrating all the changes that have been occurring on many levels, as the communities have moved into a time of managing, maintaining and sustaining all that has been built up.

Even as this process continues, however, it becomes possible to see signs of what's going to emerge in the future. What is clear is that the future development of Camphill communities has the potential to go beyond an earlier phase characterized by group consciousness and also the more contemporary process of individualization.

There is a new mood of activity and engagement beyond the traditional community boundaries. The communities are working in collaboration with parents and friends and with professional and voluntary organizations. They are developing innovative and responsive projects and initiatives. There is also a renewed interest in issues to do with ecological building, energy use and environmental sustainability. New organizational structures have emerged that are flexible and responsive and that promote inclusion, empowerment and initiative.

There has been a realization that individualization means far more than each person doing as they wish, and more about each individual taking initiative out of a sense of moral responsibility towards the community as a whole, and towards their own learning and development.

As the Camphill Movement reflects on seventy years of achievements, this might be a moment in its history when it begins to develop a renewed vision of what Camphill is and what it is striving to achieve in the 21st century — both in terms of its role as a care provider to those with disabilities and its role in society.

At this point in the development of Camphill there needs to be a process of reflection and of coming to terms with the situation as it is today. This in turn can lead to a process of beginning to envisage what will be needed in the future.

The core vision of creating community as a place for healing, transformation and renewal for both the individual and for society will depend for its continued effectiveness and vitality more than ever on the inspiration, creativity, enthusiasm and skills of each person living and working in Camphill.

It is no longer enough for the communities to trust that they can live off what has been achieved in the past. Different communities in different regions find themselves in different situations. There will no longer be universal insights that apply across the whole Camphill Movement. Each community will need to create its own future, through responding to the needs of the people in their communities and to their local and particular situations. In this process they will be able to find confidence through building on what has been achieved in the past, through a common sense of identity and through associative networks of support. However, the future will be a time of creativity and innovation, determined less by tradition and conformity and more by initiative and positive engagement in finding new ways forward.

In order to come nearer to fulfilling the true potential of what community can be, there will need to be a willingness to come to terms with the shadow side of community — the disappointments, the hardships and also the failures of community life. This recognition can lead to renewed efforts to create supportive and healthy social relationships and to engender respect for each individual on their life's path. And for their part, each individual can only live up to the real challenge of community when they have began their own personal journey of self-discovery, self-awareness and self-development.

An essential part of community life has always been celebration — as part of the rhythm of the Christian year but also more spontaneously to mark special occasions and to give expression to the joy and delight that can rise out of a shared life and common work. When people tire of tradition a new sense of creativity and inspiration is called for in order to breathe new life into these uplifting aspects of community. In the same way, renewed efforts are also needed to create a living awareness and connection to the working of the spirit into communal life. In Camphill there has always been the understanding that if people come together and create communities that seek to work for the betterment of the world, then these communities will receive help in this task from the spirit world. The insights of anthroposophy are a guide to new ways of understanding and connecting to the spiritual in the world, but never in the sense of adhering to a dogmatic belief system or a religion. Anthroposophy seeks to heighten the universal aspects of Christianity and to transcend the divisive aspects of different beliefs and worldviews.

There are signs that in the future people in Camphill communities will be less drawn to the more esoteric and formalized expressions of spirituality and more open to spiritual celebrations that are inclusive and of a more universal nature.

As society in general seems to move towards a more secular and materialistic outlook, it will become increasingly important that the individuals in communities, and the communities themselves, nurture a renewed commitment to spiritual development and awareness and to creating social, cultural and spiritual forms that enable the collaboration between this world and the spiritual world to become active and manifest.

A willingness to learn new skills to create community in more diverse situations and beyond traditional boundaries is crucial to the future development of communities. Up until recently, communities have been engaged in creating community among people who had made a definite commitment to living in Camphill and who shared a common belief in anthroposophy. Now the communities face the much harder task of nurturing a sense of community in situations of increased complexity and diversity and among a wider range of people. This is a greater challenge for Camphill but it also represents a step in the direction of sharing the lessons and gifts of community with society at large as the communities become yet more open and more engaged in the world.

For seventy years Camphill has nurtured an awareness of the innate dignity and the spiritual essence in each human being and worked to uphold this. Camphill has worked to bring about healing — healing for the individual, for the earth and for society, and has been inspired by the vision and ideals of creating a new and better world for the future.

The future development of Camphill is going to depend on a sense of confidence in what has been achieved in the past and equally a sense of certainty that the world needs community today and for the future. This confidence and the willingness to develop community in more challenging circumstances will ensure that Camphill will continue to uphold the ideals of personal transformation and social renewal, and will continue to develop the potential for community to become the social form of the future.

The Contributors

Francis Aradhya was born in Holland in 1962 and came to India in 1997 to join the Friends of Camphill India in establishing a residential community in Bangalore. She is a qualified curative educator and social therapist.

Jan Martin Bang, born in Norway, grew up in England and lived for sixteen years as a kibbutz member in Israel before joining Camphill Solborg in Norway. He is now a close neighbour of Solborg and writes about community and the environment.

Simon Beckett has been a Camphill co-worker since 1982 and lives in Newton Dee Community, Aberdeen.

Richard Blake has been a co-worker for many years at Camphill Botswana.

Friedwart Bock joined the first Camphill Seminar for Curative Education in 1949, following Waldorf, state school and paramilitary service. He is active in teaching and administration and latterly in the Karl König Archive.

Hetty v. Brandenburg has lived in Camphill in Ireland since 1976, in Glencraig and in Clanabogan. She enjoys being part of the Camphill village impulse in a variety of ways.

John Byrde, born 1943, joined the Camphill Movement in 1963 at Ringwood and Camphill Schools, Aberdeen. He moved to Perceval at St Prex, Switzerland, in 1968, and on to Romania at Casa Rozei, Urlati, in 1993.

Ursula Chowdhury is German by birth and has lived in India since 1957. She is the co-founder of the Camphill community in Bangalore and president of the Friends of Camphill India Trust.

Vasant Deshpande has been associated with Sadhana Village since its inception in 1994.

Mischa Fekete has been a co-worker/houseparent in Camphill in Ireland doing many different things for over twenty years, among them being a member of the Movement Group.

Vivian Griffiths has lived in Botton Village, had the fortune to help start Larchfield Community near Middlesbrough in 1986, and been part of Camphill Houses Stourbridge from 1996 to 2009. Now living in Cumbria he is, along with Lesley his wife, involved in holidays with people from Camphill.

Colin Haldane first met Camphill in the early seventies in Aberdeen. Having lived in Camphill communities in Ireland, Norway, England and Scotland, he now lives at Newton Dee Community, Aberdeen. Colin is a member of the Camphill Movement Core Group.

Diedra Heitzman loves her life in Camphill because she is able to accompany so many fascinating people on life journeys, has learned about things she never expected to learn, has seen first-hand the power of community and the fruits of anthroposophy, and has seemingly endless opportunities to express ideas and learn more. She has been a member of Camphill Village Kimberton Hills since 1983.

Ludwig Kraus is a senior co-worker in the Camphill Community Tapola, Finland, where he has lived since 1987. He is involved in the Northern European region and especially it´s eastern communities.

Christof-Andreas Lindenberg has been involved with Camphill since 1950, working closely with Karl König for about ten years in Scotland and Ireland, in both schools and villages. He now leads the Dorian School of Music within Camphill USA.

Michael Luxford was born England in 1946 and joined the Mount Community in Sussex in 1971.He became involved with youth guidance, moving to the Pennine Camphill Community in Yorkshire in 1980. In 1993 he initiated the Fundamental Social Law Research Group, which led to the founding of Directions for Change and in 2005 the publication of A Sense for Community.

Neil MacLean has been in Camphill in Ireland for most of the last twenty years, mainly as a gardener and houseparent.

Angelika Monteux has been a co-worker in the Camphill Rudolf Steiner schools since 1973; she has been a teacher and houseparent and is now involved with the BA Honours in Curative Education and Social Pedagogy in partnership with the University of Aberdeen.

Cornelius Pietzner serves as Treasurer on the Executive Council of the General Anthroposophical Society at the Goetheanum in Switzerland. Born in Northern Ireland, Pietzner was raised in Camphill in the United States and later founded a Camphill community. He was also President of the Camphill Association of North America. His interests lie particularly in the area of social finance, entrepreneurship and community building.

Andrew Plant has lived for thirty years in Camphill communities in Northern Ireland and Scotland.

Russel Pooler was born in California in 1954 and joined Camphill Delrow in the mid-seventies. He is a Waldorf schoolteacher, eurythmist, playwright and lives in the Newton Dee Camphill Community.

Penelope Roberts, New York, came to Camphill as a young adult in 1970 and has been active in the Camphill outreach in India since 1990. She is currently director of the training course in social therapy in Copake and is active in the Athroposophical Society in America as well as Asia.

Karin von Schilling has been in Camphill since 1951, first in Scotland, England, Ireland, then as a pioneer in South Africa where she lived for many years. Her general anthroposophical work took her to many other parts of Africa.

Julian Sleigh was born in 1927 in Florence, schooling and university in wartime England. After four years in industry he trained in curative education at Camphill, Aberdeen. In 1958 he joined the Camphill centre at Hermanus, South Africa. He was ordained priest of the Christian Community in 1965 and helped to found and develop the Camphill village near Cape Town.

Richard Steel has been a co-worker in Camphill in Germany since the early seventies. He now works for the Karl König Archives in Berlin.

Ha Vinh Tho lived and worked in a Camphill community in Perceval in Switzerland for 28 years. Together with his wife he created the Eurasia Foundation, an organisation developing curative education and social therapy in Vietnam. He is currently head of Learning and Development at the International Committee of the Red Cross (ICRC) in Geneva and a visiting professor in several universities.

Bibliography

Allen, Joan de Ris (1990) *Living Buildings*, Camphill Architects, Aberdeen, UK.

Bang, Jan Martin (2005) *Ecovillages: A Practical Guide to Sustainable Communities*, Floris Books, UK.

—, (2007) *Growing Eco-communities: Practical ways to Create Sustainability*, Floris Books, UK.

—, (2009) *The Hidden Seed: the Story of the Camphill Bible Evening*, Bright Pen Books and Authors-on-Line Ltd, UK.

Bloor, M., McKeganey, N. and Fonkert, D. (1988) *One Foot in Eden: A Sociological Study of the Range of Therapeutic Community Practice*, Routledge, UK.

Bock, Friedwart (Ed) (2004) *The Builders of Camphill: Lives and Destinies of the Founders*, Floris Books, UK.

Camphill Correspondence. For details of this magazine, see contact addresses.

Christie, Nils (1989) *Beyond Loneliness and Institutions*, Norwegian University Press.

Dietler, U. (Ed) (2006) *Anthroposophie und Buddhismus*, Rudolf Steiner Verlag, Dornach, Switzerland.

Hansmann, H. (1992) *Education for Special Needs: Principles and Practice in Camphill Schools*, Floris Books, UK.

Jackson, Robin (Ed) (2006) *Holistic Special Education: Camphill Principles and Practice*, Floris Books, UK.

König, Karl (1990) *Man as a Social Being*, Camphill Press, UK.

—, (1993) *The Camphill Movement*, Camphill Press, UK.

—, (2009) *Seeds for Social Renewal: The Camphill Village Conferences*, Floris Books, UK.

—, (2009) *The Child with Special Needs: Letters and Essays on Curative Education*, Floris Books, UK.

Luxford, M. and J. (2003) *A Sense for Community*, Directions for Change, UK.

McKanan, Dan (2007) *Touching the World: Christian Communities Transforming Society*, Liturgical Press, USA.

Morton, A. (Ed) (1998) *Beyond Fear: Vision, Hope and Generosity*, St Andrew Press, UK.

Moscoff, B., Clay, B. and colleagues (2000) *Shaping the Flame*, Camphill Foundation and Robinswood Press, UK.

Müller-Wiedemann, Hans (1996) *Karl König*, Camphill Books, UK.

Nauck, Erika (2009) *We came ... Biographical sketches of the twenty-five participants of the first Camphill Seminar in Curative Education 1949–1951.* Private publication, available from Botton Village Bookshop, UK.

Perlas, Nicanor (2003) *Shaping Globalization: Civil Society, Cultural Power, and Threefolding*, New Society Publishers, Canada.

Pietzner, Cornelius (Ed) (1990) *A Candle on the Hill — Images of Camphill Life*, Floris Books, UK.

—, (Ed) (1986) *Village Life — The Camphill Communities*, Neugebauer Press, USA.

Pooler, Russel (2009) *A Rosicrucian Soul — The Life Journey of Paul Marshall Allen*, Lindisfarne Books, USA.

Ravetz, Tom (2009) *Free from Dogma: Theological Reflections in the Christian Community*, Floris Books, UK.

Selg, Peter (Ed) (2008) *Karl König: My task*, Floris Books, UK.

—, (2008) *Karl König's Path into Anthroposophy*, Floris Books, UK.

Smith, M. (2009) *Rethinking Residential Child Care: Positive Perspectives.* The Policy Press, UK.

Stedall, Jonathan (2009) *Where on Earth is Heaven?* Hawthorn Press, UK.

Steiner, Rudolf (1998) *Education for Special Needs — the Curative Education Course*, Rudolf Steiner Press, UK.

—, (2006) *Anthroposophy and the Social Question*, Kessinger Publishing, USA.

—, (2005) *Esoteric Christianity*, Rudolf Steiner Press, UK.

—, (1983) *The Four Mystery Plays*, translated by Adam Bittleston, Rudolf Steiner Press, UK.

—, (1979) *Goethes Geistesart (The character of Goethe's spirit)*, Rudolf Steiner Verlag, Dornach, Switzerland.

—, (2009) *Riddles of the Soul*, Steiner Books, USA.

—, (1999) *Towards Social Renewal*, Rudolf Steiner Press, UK.

Surkamp, Johannes (Ed) (2007) *The Lives of Camphill: An Anthology of the Pioneers*, Floris Books, UK.

Van Diun, Veronika (2002) *A Child in Community*, Upfront Publishing, UK.

Weihs, T., revised by Hailey, A.M., Hailey, M.J. and Blitz, N.M. (1987) *Children in Need of Special Care*, Souvenir Press, UK.

Weihs, A. and Tallo, J., revised by Farrants, W. (1988) *Camphill Villages*, Camphill Press, UK.

Contact Addresses

Austria
Camphill Liebenfels
Pflausach 3, A-9556 Liebenfels
Tel: +43 (0)4215 248175/255475
Fax: +43 (0)4215 248178/255478
Email: pflausach@camphill.at

Botswana
Camphill Community Rankoromane
PO Box 2224, Gaborone
Tel: +267 5337 593
Fax: +267 5337 279
Email: camphill@info.bw

Canada
Camphill Nottawasaga
7841 4th Line, Angus, Ontario, L0M 1B1
Tel: +1 705 424 5363
Fax: +1 705 424 1854
Email: info@camphill.on.ca
Web: www.camphill.on.ca

Czech Republic
Camphill Ceské Kopisty
Ceské Kopisty 6, 41201 Litomerice
Tel/fax: +420 416 738 673
Email: camphill@camphill.cz
Web: www.camphill.cz

England
Botton Village
Danby, Whitby, North Yorkshire YO21 2NJ
Tel: +44 (0)1287 661298
Fax: +44 (0)1287 660888
Email: botton@camphill.org.uk
Web: www.camphill.org.uk

Camphill Village Trust Ltd
The Old School House, Town Street, Old Malton,
YO17 7HD
Tel: +44 (0)845 0944638
Fax: +44 (0)845 0944639
Email: cvtsec@camphill.org.uk

Estonia
Pahkla Camphilli Küla
79742 Kohila vald, Rapla maakond
Tel: +372 4897 231
Email: pahklack@hot.ee
Web: www.pahklack.ee

Finland
Sylvia-koti
Kyläkatu 140, FIN-15700 Lahti
Tel: +358 (0)3 883 130
Fax: +358 (0)3 883 1315
Email: info@sylvia-koti.fi
Web: www.syvia-koti.fi

France
Foyer de Vie: Le Béal
F-26 770 Taulignan
Tel: +33 (0)4 75 53 55 33
Fax: +33 (0)4 75 53 66 69
Email: contact@lebeal.org
Web: www.lebeal.org

Germany
Camphill Schulgemeinschaft
Föhrenbühl
Föhrenbühlweg 5, D-88633 Heiligenberg-
Steigen
Tel: +49 (0)7554 8001 0
Fax: +49 (0)7554 80011 63
Email: info@foehrenbuehl.de
Web: www.foehrenbuehl.de

Hungary
Velem Camphill Community
H-9726, Velem, Kossuth u. 1. Hungary
Tel/fax: +36 (0)30 95 12 455
Email: camphill.velem@t-online.hu
Web: www.camphill.hu

Ireland
Camphill Community Duffcarrig
Gorey, Co. Wexford
Tel: +353 (0)53 94 25911
Fax: +353 (0)53 94 25910
Email: duffcarrig@camphill.ie
Web: www.camphill.ie

Latvia
Camphill Village Rozkalni
p.n.Lizdeni, Valmieras raj. LV 4231 Latvia
Tel/fax: +371 423 3210
Email: rozkalni@apollo.lv

Netherlands
Camphill Gemeenschap
Christophorus
Duinweg 35, NL-3735 LC Bosch en Duin
Tel: +31 (0)30 69 35 222
Fax: +31 (0)30 69 31 117
Email: info@christophorus.nl
Web: www.christophorus.nl

Northern Ireland
Camphill Community Glencraig
Craigavad, Holywood, Co. Down BT18 ODB
Tel: +44 (0)28 9042 3396
Fax: +44 (0)28 9042 8199
Email: office@glencraig.org.uk
Web: www.glencraig.org.uk

Norway
Vidaråsen Landsby
N-3158 Andebu
Tel (am only): +47 33 44 41 00
Fax: +47 33 44 41 01
Email: office@vidaraasen.no
Web: www.camphill.no/vidaraasen

Central Secretariat for Camphill Village Trust in Norway
Reidar Jensensgate 10
N-7550 Hommelvik
Tel: +47 73 97 84 60
Email: landsbystiftelsen@camphill.no
Web: www.camphill.no

Poland
Wspólnota w Wójtówce
Wójtówka 1, PL-57 540 Ladek Zdroj
Tel/fax: +48 (0)74 8146 501

Russia
Camphill Village Svetlana
Alexina Village, Volchov, 187439 St Petersburg
Tel: +7 813 633 8760
Email: dsvet1@yandex.ru
Web: www.camphillsvetlana.org

Scotland
Newton Dee Community
Newton Dee, Bieldside, Aberdeen AB15 9DX
Tel: +44 (0)1224 868701
Fax: +44 (0)1224 869398
Email: info@newtondee.org.uk
Web: www.newtondee.org.uk

Association of Camphill Communities
Murtle House, Bieldside, Aberdeen AB15 9EP
Tel: +44 (0)1224 867658
Email: camphill.association@camphill.net
Web: www.camphill-uk-ireland.net

Camphill Foundation UK
Newton Dee Community, Bieldside, Aberdeen
AB15 9DX
Tel: +44 (0)1224 868701
Fax: +44 (0)1224 869398

South Africa
Camphill Farm Community
PO Box 301, Hermanus 7200, Western Cape
Tel: +27 (0)28 313 8200
Fax: +27 (0)28 313 8210
Email: info@camphill-hermanus.org.za
Web: www.camphill-hermanus.org.za

Sweden
Staffansgårdens Camphill
bygemenskap
Furugatan 1, SE-82060 Delsbo
Tel: +46 (0)653 168 50
Fax: +46 (0)653 109 68
Email: info@staffansgarden.com
Web: www.staffansgarden.com

Switzerland
Fondation Perceval
Route de Lussy 45, CH 1162 St Prex
Tel: +41 (0)21 823 11 11
Fax: +41 (0)21 823 11 22
Email: info@perceval.ch
Web: www.perceval.ch

USA
Camphill Village USA, Inc.
84 Camphill Road, Copake, NY 12516
Tel: +1 518 329 4851/7924
Fax: +1 518 329 0377
Email: cvinfo@camphillvillage.org
Web: www.camphillvillage.org

Camphill Association of North America
84 Camphill Road, Copake, NY 12516
Tel: +1 518 329 4851
Fax: +1 518 329 0377
Email: info@camphill.org
Web: www.camphill.org

Wales
Coleg Elidyr Camphill Communities
Rhandirmwyn, Llandovery, Carmarthenshire
SA20 0NL
Tel: +44 (0)1550 760400
Fax: +44 (0)1550 760331
Email: admin@colegelidyr.com

Other useful contacts

Karl König Archive
Camphill House, Milltimber, Aberdeen AB13 0AN
Email: aberdeen@karl-koenig-archive.net
Web: www.karl-koenig-archive.net

Berlin Office
Finckensteinalle 1, D-12205 Berlin
Contact: R Steel
Tel: +49 (0)30 6174 14 14
Fax: +49 (0)30 6174 14 15
Email: r.steel@karl-koenig-archive.net

Camphill Correspondence
Editorial: Maria Mountain
37 Highfield Road, Halesowen, West Midlands
B63 2DH
Tel: +44 (0)1384 569153
Email: maria.mntn@gmail.com

Subscriptions: Bianca Hügel
34 Wheeler Street, Stourbridge, West Midlands
DY8 1XJ
Tel: +44 (0)1384 375931
Email: bianca.huegel@gmail.com

*European Cooperation in Anthroposophical
Curative Education and Social Therapy*
Postbus 560, NL-3700 AN Zeist, Netherlands
Tel: +31 (0)30 694 55 40
Fax: +31 (0)30 694 55 90
Email: ecce@ecce.eu
Web: www.ecce.eu

Friends of Camphill India
19th km Bannerghatta Road, Bangalore 560 083
Email: campindia@hotmail.com
Web: www.friends-of-camphill-india.com

Picture Acknowledgments

Chapters 1 & 2
Karl König Archives: photos
Günther Lehr: hand-drawn map of Camphill

Chapter 3
Karl König Archives: photos

Chapter 4
Roland Bienoth: 130 bottom, 131top
Paul Bock: 130 top
Georg Domeier: 132 bottom right
Boris Moscoff: 110, 115, 127, 132 bottom left
Nick Poole: 100, 103, 104, 106, 120, 126, 129, 132

Chapter 5
Jan Martin Bang: Scotland, Le Béal, Ceske Kópisty, Hungary, Solborg
Sarah Maria Bass: Botswana
Borgny Berglund: Jøssåsen, Vallersund, Vidaråsen
Camphill Scottish Region Archive: Scotland
Camphill North American Archive: USA
Vasant Deshpande: Sadhana Village
Stefan Eberle: Solborg
Karl König Archives: Germany, Austria, Humanus House Switzerland, Perceval
Olga Kuolikova: Vidaråsen
Neil MacLean: Ireland
Ikuko Tsuchiya: Botton Village

ISBN 978-086315-607-6

The Lives of Camphill
An Anthology of the Pioneers

COMPILED AND EDITED BY JOHANNES M SURKAMP

Gathered together here are 129 short biographies and photographs spanning thirty years. Each tells a fascinating individual story, and together they form a remarkable whole, documenting the history of Camphill in the most appropriate way: through its people.

ISBN 978-086315-442-3

The Builders of Camphill
Lives and Destinies of the Founders

EDITED BY FRIEDWART BOCK

This is the story of Camphill's eleven intrepid founders. Alix Roth had worked as a photographer in Vienna; Anke Weihs was a dancer; Thomas Weihs had studied medicine in Vienna and Basel; Carlo Pietzner was an artist in Vienna; and Peter Roth began medical studies and later became a priest. This book documents how these and other diverse talents came together to form a network which now numbers over 100 homes, schools and villages.

www.florisbooks.co.uk